The Country Life Book of the
ROYAL SILVER JUBILEE

The Country Life Book of the
ROYAL SILVER JUBILEE

Patrick Montague-Smith

COUNTRY LIFE BOOKS

CONTENTS

half title *Off-duty scene photographed at Balmoral by Patrick Lichfield as the Queen sets off to exercise her dogs.*

title spread *The Queen acknowledges the crowd as the Irish State Coach carries her to the state opening of Parliament in October 1969.*

this page *Standing before a painting of Windsor Castle where the Garter ceremony is held each year, the Queen displays the robes of the Sovereign of the Order.*

FOREWORD 7

ELIZABETH BECOMES QUEEN 9

FIRST YEARS OF THE NEW REIGN 29

EVENTS OF THE SIXTIES 51

THE CONTEMPORARY SEVENTIES 79

THE WORK OF A SOVEREIGN 103

PHILIP THE QUEEN'S CONSORT 115

THE ROYAL CHILDREN 135

THE QUEEN MOTHER 159

THE ROYAL FAMILY TREE 174

ACKNOWLEDGEMENTS 176

Published for Country Life Books by
The Hamlyn Publishing Group Limited
London · New York · Sydney · Toronto
Astronaut House, Feltham, Middlesex
Copyright © The Hamlyn Publishing Group Limited 1976
First published 1976
Eleventh Impression 1977

ISBN 0 600 38200 1

Illustrations reproduced by Metric Reproductions Ltd, Chelmsford, Essex

Printed Offset Litho and bound in Great Britain by
Cox & Wyman Ltd, London, Fakenham and Reading

FOREWORD

As Earl Marshal, Miles
Fitzalan Howard, seventeenth
Duke of Norfolk, is responsible
for organizing state occasions. He
is the Premier Duke and Earl of
England, and one of the Queen's
Great Officers of State.

Arundel Castle

The Silver Jubilee of the accession of Her Majesty The Queen is a joyful occasion which calls for an expression of gratitude and for our prayers. Rejoicing that Her reign has been a time when our country has not been involved in a war; thankfulness for the example which Her Majesty and her family have set in the way of service to other people in so many directions; our prayers that Her Majesty and all the Royal Family may long continue to be safe from harm when discontent is all too common.

On Coronation Day, 2 June 1953, Sir Winston Churchill said: ''We love Her as Queen, and we love her for herself'' I echo this tribute, and am honoured to write a Foreword to this book which marks a quarter of a century's reign by a Sovereign whose graciousness is unparalleled and whose devotion to duty reminds us all how much we owe to Her.

Norfolk.

ELIZABETH BECOMES QUEEN

The 1936 abdication crisis gave a severe jolt to the British monarchy and made the task of the new King, George VI, extremely difficult. When Edward VIII renounced the throne after an eleven-month reign, his brother was appalled at the prospect of taking over. He was not strong, he had a voice impediment, and above all he felt untrained for the task. He confessed to his cousin Lord Louis Mountbatten, 'Dickie, this is absolutely terrible . . . I am quite unprepared for it . . . I've never seen a state paper. I'm only a naval officer, it's the only thing I know about'. Lord Mountbatten told him that oddly, when George V had succeeded his father, and his elder brother the Duke of Clarence was dead, he had said almost the same words to Mountbatten's father, who had replied, 'George, you're wrong. There is no more fitting preparation for a King than to have been trained in the Navy'.

George VI was greatly helped by his Queen, whom he had married in Westminster Abbey in 1923, when he was Duke of York, and he subsequently made considerable progress in overcoming his voice impediment with the help of a brilliant young speech therapist called Lionel Logue. But Britain under his reign was soon to be plunged into the Munich crisis, and the war with Germany and Japan that ensued. Then came the problems of the postwar period. This succession of events was bound to strain the health of one who had never been strong.

April 1948 saw the King and Queen celebrating their silver wedding at a service of thanksgiving in St Paul's Cathedral. That November a son, Prince Charles, was born to the King's elder daughter, Princess Elizabeth, and her husband, Prince Philip. Succession was thus assured to the second generation, but a bulletin on 23rd November announced that the King's ill health prevented him from undertaking the proposed royal tour to Australia and New Zealand, and it was agreed that Princess Elizabeth and Prince Philip should go in his place. In March the following year the King underwent an operation to improve the blood supply to his right foot.

After the pageantry surrounding the Festival of Britain in May 1951 the King's illness recurred, and eventually his doctors confirmed that he was suffering from a malignant growth. They agreed that, despite a risk to his heart, there was no alternative but to operate for the removal of his left lung. He

was not told he had cancer, but he accepted the situation. The operation, his fifth, was performed on Sunday 23rd September, and was successful.

The King's recovery met with universal rejoicing, and he once again immersed himself in his work. The general election in October brought Winston Churchill back as Prime Minister in place of the Labour leader, Clement Attlee. The King and Queen were invited by the South African Government on a private visit for him to recuperate, and plans were made to leave on 10th March.

As usual the royal family spent Christmas at Sandringham. The King was spared the task of a 'live' Christmas Day broadcast in the tradition started by his father. Instead, the speech was recorded piece by piece as his strength allowed. In comparison with the broadcasts of previous years the result was disappointing and the nation was shocked by the King's evident weakness. Even so, when examined by his doctors at Buckingham Palace on 29th January, the King's progress was pronounced satisfactory.

left *The supreme moment of the coronation at Westminster Abbey on 2nd June 1953.*

right *In this happy study of King George VI in July 1946, he enjoys a joke with his elder daughter, Princess Elizabeth, outside the Royal Lodge, Windsor.*

On the following day, for the first time since his illness, he and the royal family spent an evening at the theatre and saw the musical *South Pacific* at Drury Lane. This was partly to celebrate his recovery, but chiefly to say farewell to Princess Elizabeth and Prince Philip, who were flying to Kenya the next day to begin a tour which was to take them to East Africa and then on to Australia and New Zealand.

On a cold and dreary January day the King travelled to London Airport to say goodbye to his daughter and son-in-law. Millions of people saw the farewell scenes on the newsreel. As he stood, hatless in the biting wind, sadly watching Elizabeth's plane move along the runway, many imagined that this might

above King George VI, with Queen Elizabeth and the royal family, receiving a great ovation on the occasion of their silver wedding on 26th April 1948. On the left of the balcony at Buckingham Palace are Prince Philip, Princess Elizabeth, and the Duke and Duchess of Gloucester, and on the right Princess Margaret and Queen Mary.
left King George VI waves his last goodbye to his daughter at London Airport on the start of her Commonwealth tour. Six days later, on 6th February 1952, he died at Sandringham.
above right Princess Elizabeth at Sagana Lodge in Kenya with Sir Philip Mitchell, Governor. This photograph was taken on the day she received the sad news that her father had died.
far right In another scene from those few days spent in Kenya, Princess Elizabeth meets Prince Bin Salim, born on the same day as Prince Charles.

be the last time he would ever see her.

Knowing that Elizabeth and Philip would be visiting Kenya, Captain Sherbrooke Walker and his wife Lady Bettie, who ran the Outspan Hotel, Nyeri, invited them to stay a night in the celebrated Treetops, a small observation lodge built high up in a fig tree, to watch and photograph the wild game below. The visit was arranged for 5th February. The presence of dangerous game was to be signalled by Lady Bettie placing a white flag on the roof of the observation lodge as a warning.

At about three o'clock the royal cars arrived at the edge of the forest. From here a path only a few feet wide extended to Treetops, a quarter of a mile away. As the party made their way through the bush, the trumpeting of elephants was heard, getting louder and louder. Philip was asked to decide whether the party should continue or turn back. 'Go ahead', he whispered. To reduce numbers Lady Pamela Mountbatten and Philip's secretary, Commander Mike Parker, climbed two of the safety ladders placed along the path.

When Philip, Elizabeth and the rest were within fifty yards of Treetops, the whole herd was seen, but as there was a cross-wind the big cow facing them did not pick up their scent. Captain Walker sighed with relief as the couple climbed up the thirty-five foot ladder to safety.

The Princess spent most of that night on the balcony watching the animals below by floodlight. At dawn she was up again, filming a rhinoceros.

The visit was over at about nine o'clock on the following morning, when the party walked back to the cars. Captain

Walker told the Princess, 'If you have the same courage, Ma'am, in facing what the future sends you as you have in facing an elephant at eight yards, we are going to be fortunate indeed'. The party then returned to the Royal Lodge at Sagana.

In the meantime at Sandringham, on 5th February, the King was enjoying the sort of day he liked best, having decided to go out for some rough shooting. It was a perfect day later described by Winston Churchill as 'a happy day of sunshine and sport'. With Lord Fermoy, his friend and neighbour, and a party of five guns, the King drove out to the Flitcham beat on the royal estate before ten o'clock that morning. For six hours, with only one stop for a picnic lunch in the village hall, the party tramped over the frosty fields. During the shoot the King bagged nine hares and brought down a pigeon. He bade farewell to the others, saying, 'Well, it's been a very good day's sport, gentlemen. I will expect you here at nine o'clock on Thursday.' He had arranged another shoot for the next day.

The Queen and Princess Margaret spent the afternoon cruising on the Norfolk Broads and visiting Ludham to see Edward Seago's paintings. At dinner the King joked and discussed the day's incidents. By coincidence, Lady Bettie Walker's brother-in-law was a guest, and told the King and Queen about Treetops.

Twice during the evening the King went out to the kennels to look at his golden retriever, Roddy, who had a thorn in his paw. After dinner he listened to Princess Margaret playing the piano, did a bit to his crossword, and at ten o'clock heard the latest news of Princess Elizabeth's tour. At about half past ten he went to bed in his room on the ground floor, which he had used since his illness.

The footman, Daniel Long, took him up a cup of cocoa at eleven o'clock, and found him in bed reading a sports magazine. The King wished him a cheerful goodnight. About midnight a watchman outside noticed that he was fixing the latch of his window. At half past seven in the morning the assistant valet, James Macdonald, began to run the King's bath, then went into the bedroom with the early morning tea. When he drew the curtains, the King, normally a light sleeper, did not stir. He had died in his sleep. Macdonald immediately informed an officer of the Household; and a lady in waiting carried the news to the Queen and Princess Margaret. The King's physician, Dr James Ansell, was sent for and he confirmed that the King had died some hours before, probably soon after midnight, from a coronary thrombosis. He was aged fifty-six.

Within an hour of the royal party's return to Sagana for the last day's break in the official programme, Commander Mike Parker, Philip's secretary, received an urgent telephone call from the Outspan Hotel. Major Charteris, the Princess's private secretary, was on the line.

above left *On 7th February 1952, the new Queen Elizabeth II, emerges alone from the aircraft that overnight had brought her back from Kenya on the sudden death of her father. Formally waiting in line to meet her are her Prime Minister, Winston Churchill, Clement Attlee and Lord Mountbatten.*
left *Standing alone and silent for a brief moment while others talk, Elizabeth remains dignified at this time of personal grief.*
right *The Queen passing through the ranks of the Yeoman of the Guard after distributing the maundy money at Westminster Abbey on 10th April 1952 – the first public engagement of her reign.*

above *On coronation day 1953, a contingent of the Royal Canadian Mounted Police pass in procession along the Mall under the triumphant arches. They received a tremendous welcome from the crowds (right) whose spirits remained undampened after many patient hours of waiting in the rain.*

above right *The Queen and her consort Prince Philip leave Buckingham Palace in the magnificent golden state coach drawn by eight greys with four mounted and capped postilions.*

A reporter of the *East African Standard* had told him that the King was dead. The news had been picked up by his paper in Nairobi from a Reuter's message. It was then half past one, local time.

Philip was taking a short siesta in his bedroom when Commander Parker tapped on his door. Without his usual cheerfulness, he told Philip, 'I'm afraid there's some awful news. The King is dead.' Later he recalled, 'I never felt so sorry for anyone in my life. He looked as if you'd dropped half the world on him.' The two desperately twiddled the knobs of their radio hoping to hear a news-flash, but the only clue as to what had happened was a series of programmes of solemn music.

For an hour Philip kept the secret to himself: he refused to tell his wife until he had received confirmation. Elizabeth was suggesting plans for the following day. He made an excuse to get her away from the telephone into the garden, but soon afterwards she returned to her room to write her correspondence. Philip at last obtained confirmation of the news from London, and now told the Princess that her father was dead. For the

first time since Queen Victoria's death in 1901, half a century ago, the sovereign was a woman, the sixth queen regnant in England's history.

A plaque was later fixed to the Treetops fig tree commemorating Elizabeth's accession: 'In this Mgumu Tree Her Royal Highness the Princess Elizabeth and His Royal Highness the Duke of Edinburgh spent the night of February 5th 1952. While here Princess Elizabeth succeeded to the throne through the death of her father King George the Sixth.'

The new Queen immediately returned home from Kenya. After the 4,000-mile flight, delayed by a tropical thunderstorm, she was met at London Airport in the darkness of the evening of 7th February by her prime minister, Winston Churchill, the leader of the opposition, Clement Attlee, and other ministers. Also there were her uncle the Duke of Gloucester, and Philip's uncle and aunt, Lord and Lady Mountbatten. The size of the party was cut down on the express order of the Prime Minister, as a gesture of respect on this poignant occasion.

Prince Philip waited in the plane for a few moments to allow

top and right *The Queen is crowned. As the Crown of St Edward is placed on her head, peers and peeresses in the congregation don their coronets.*

above *The Queen receives the kiss of fealty from her husband.*

the Queen, making a striking impression in deep mourning, to come down the steps to greet her waiting ministers. It was just one week since she had left. She then returned to the capital to console her mother, Elizabeth the Queen Mother. Over the Queen's home in London, Clarence House, the royal standard flew for the first time, and almost immediately Elizabeth had to preside over a Privy Council meeting.

On the following day, from the balcony of St James's Palace, and accompanied by a fanfare from four state trumpeters, the Garter King of Arms proclaimed her Elizabeth II, by the style of 'by the Grace of God, Queen of this Realm and of all her other Realms and Territories Head of the Commonwealth, Defender of the Faith'. Similar proclamations were made at three other places in London, in other cities and towns in Britain and the Commonwealth, and aboard Her Majesty's ships 'wherever they might be'.

The new Queen was aged twenty-five. Her private existence as a young married woman with two children had come abruptly to an end. Although she had received some training as the heiress presumptive to the throne, and though she and Prince Philip had done much to help her parents, particularly during the King's illness, there was an enormous amount to learn. She spent long hours studying state documents and enacting the duties of a hardworking sovereign.

Meanwhile the day of her coronation drew nearer. Preparations for this elaborate ceremony had started almost immediately. Overall responsibility for the organization fell to the late Duke of Norfolk, who held the hereditary office of earl marshal. This was his second coronation, and he carried it out faultlessly after sixteen months of detailed planning.

The Coronation Commission was set up in April 1952 under the chairmanship of Prince Philip. Among the complex problems which had to be decided was that of Philip's role in the processions. Should he have a coach to himself, travel with the Queen, or ride on horseback? Queen Anne was the only previous Queen regnant to have had a prince consort, Prince George of Denmark, but her example offered no answer, for she suffered so badly from gout that she had to be carried to the Abbey in a low chair.

Two months later, the coronation date was proclaimed as 2nd June 1953, and the Court of Claims was set up. This always sits before a coronation, and adjudicates on the various duties to be performed at the ceremony.

The Queen and Prince Philip daily discussed all the coronation problems. They decided to lengthen the route to accommodate the many thousands of children wanting to see the processions, and opposed the original suggestion by the committee of the Coronation Commission, that the ceremony should not be televised. The Abbey was closed and the keys handed over by the Dean to the Earl Marshal. Seating had to be erected for over 7,000 people, and a special annexe built outside the west door. Over 2,000 square yards of carpet were required for the Abbey and the annexe. The Imperial State Gown had to be remodelled for the Queen and the State Coach built for George III in 1761, in which she was to travel to and from the Abbey, had to be renovated and regilded.

Decorations appeared on public buildings, and in the streets on 10th May, these including three sixty-five foot triumphal arches in the Mall. Stands were erected for over 100,000 people containing 700 miles of tubular scaffolding. Souvenirs flooded into the shops. Mugs and pictures showing Prince Philip as a

above *At the horse trials at Badminton in April 1953, the royal party takes to the grass. With the Queen can be seen the Queen Mother, Princess Margaret and the Princess Royal, together with the Duke of Beaufort, the Queen's Master of the Horse.*

right *On another equestrian occasion, this time at Royal Ascot in June 1958, the royal group comprises the Queen and Queen Mother, the Princess Royal, Duchess of Gloucester, Princess Margaret and Prince Philip.*

left *In her progress down the Nave of Westminster Abbey after the coronation ceremony, the Queen, flanked by her Maids of Honour, carries the sceptre in her right hand, the orb in her left and wears the Imperial State Crown.*

above and right *As vast crowds throng the gates in their excitement after the great event, the Queen makes one of many appearances on the balcony at Buckingham Palace with the royal family. She is still wearing the Imperial State Crown.*

left *The state opening of Parliament was televised and photographed for the first time on 28th October 1958. In this photograph by Cecil Beaton, the Queen reads her speech from the throne while in front of the dais, on the left, Lord Home holds the cap of maintenance and on the right, Viscount Montgomery holds the heavy sword of state.*

The royal group in the Throne Room at Buckingham Palace after the coronation. The members of the group are as follows:

front row 1 *Prince Michael of Kent.* 2 *Prince Charles.* 3 *Princess Anne.* 4 *Prince Richard of Gloucester.* 5 *Prince William of Gloucester.*

second row 6 *The Duchess of Beaufort.* 7 *The Hereditary Grand Duchess of Luxembourg.* 8 *Princess Marie Louise.* 9 *Princess Alice, Countess of Athlone.* 10 *Princess Alexandra of Kent.* 11 *The Duchess of Kent.* 12 *The Crown Princess of Norway.* 13 *The Princess Margaret.* 14 *The Queen.* 15 *Queen Elizabeth the Queen Mother.* 16 *The Princess Royal.* 17 *The Duchess of Gloucester.* 18 *Lady Patricia Ramsay.* 19 *Countess Mountbatten.* 20 *Earl Mountbatten.* 21 *Lady Pamela Mountbatten.* 22 *Lady Brabourne.* 23 *Princess George of Greece.* 24 *Prince George of Greece.*

third row 25 *The Hereditary Grand Duke of Luxembourg.* 26 *The Prince of Liege.* 27 *The Duke of Beaufort.* 28 *Lt. Col. Sir Henry Abel Smith.* 29 *The Duke of Kent.* 30 *Lady May Abel Smith.* 31 *The Crown Prince of Norway.* 32 *Princess Astrid of Norway.* 33 *Princess Dorothea of Hesse.* 34 *The Duke of Edinburgh.* 35 *The Marchioness of Cambridge.* 36 *The Duke of Gloucester.* 37 *The Earl of Harewood.* 38 *The Honourable Gerald Lascelles.* 39 *The Countess of Harewood.* 40 *Captain Alexander Ramsay.* 41 *Admiral The Honourable Alexander Ramsay.* 42 *Mr Peter Whitley (husband of the Lady Mary Whitley, nee Cambridge).* 43 *Lord Brabourne.*

fourth row 44 *The Prince Axel of Denmark.* 45 *Princess Margaretha of Denmark.* 46 *Prince Kraft of Hohenlohe-Langenburg.* 47 *The Princess of Hohenlohe-Langenburg (immediately on the right of the Duke of Edinburgh).* 48 *The Prince of the Netherlands.* 49 *The Margrave of Baden.* 50 *The Margravine of Baden.* 51 *Princess Christina of Hesse.* 52 *The Earl of Athlone.* 53 *Prince Max of Baden.* 54 *The Prince of Hohenlohe-Langenburg.*

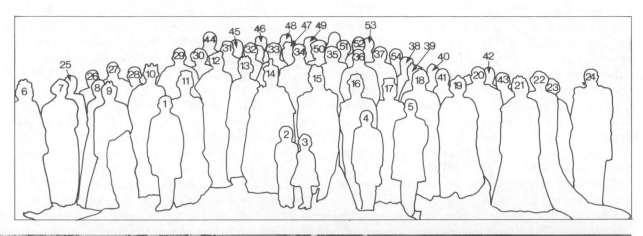

commander later became collectors' pieces, for he was promoted to the rank of admiral of the fleet too late for the trade to make alterations.

When it came, coronation day proved to be both dull and wet, but nothing could dampen the ardour of the waiting throngs eager to see a spectacle last witnessed sixteen years earlier when the Queen's father had been crowned.

The first procession left at eight o'clock in the morning, when the Lord Mayor of London set out from Mansion House in his famous gilded coach, surrounded by pikemen. Almost an hour later ten cars brought the first members of the royal family from Buckingham Palace to the Abbey, and members of the diplomatic corps from St James's Palace.

There were five processions to the Abbey, headed by the colonial rulers. Then followed the nine carriages of the prime ministers from the Commonwealth, the Princes and Princesses from the Palace, and the speaker's coach on its short journey from the House of Commons. At ten o'clock the Queen Mother's procession left Clarence House, she and Princess Margaret in the Irish State Coach raising a special cheer from the crowds.

The excitement was intense when, twenty minutes later, the magnificent royal State Coach passed through the gates of Buckingham Palace at walking pace. It was drawn by eight Windsor greys, caparisoned in state harness and controlled by four postillions in dark velvet caps and gold braid jackets, accompanied by red-coated footmen and yeomen of the guard. Inside were the Queen, in a white silk gown designed by Norman Hartnell and embroidered with commonwealth emblems, and Prince Philip wearing the full-dress uniform of an

admiral of the fleet. The couple waved to the cheering onlookers on their journey to the Abbey.

A fanfare of trumpets heralded the Queen's arrival at the Abbey. The procession, marshalled in the annexe, moved up the nave, and as the Queen passed the organ screen and came into the view of the forty Westminster scholars above, she was greeted, according to established custom, with their shouts of 'Vivat Regina Elizabeth! Vivat! Vivat! Vivat!'

There are four main phases in the coronation ceremony: the recognition; the oath; the communion service, during which the anointing, crowning and enthroning take place; and finally the homage. During the recognition, a survival of the ancient practice of election of the sovereign, the archbishop, with the great officers of state, went in turn to the east, west, and north of the 'theatre', the central part of the Abbey. Each time the archbishop called upon the assembly, 'Sirs, I here present to you Queen Elizabeth your undoubted Queen,' to which the congregation answered, 'God Save Queen Elizabeth'. The Queen stood in full view by the coronation chair, facing each side in turn.

Then came the pledging of the oath, which affirms that the sovereign is subject to the law and must govern according to the law. The Queen answered the archbishop's questions and signed the oath, which had been amended since the previous coronation due to commonwealth changes.

The ensuing communion service began with the annointing, when the Queen dedicated herself to the service of her people and was consecrated with Holy oil. With the sword of state carried before her, the Queen, having discarded her robes, was now in a plain white garment. She moved to be seated for the

first time in the coronation chair, made by Edward I to display the historic Stone of Scone. The canopy of cloth of gold was held over her by four garter knights to conceal her from the sight of the congregation, while the archbishop dipped his thumb into the Holy oil and annointed her upon the hands, breast and head. Then she was presented with the Holy Bible by the Scottish Moderator performing this duty for the first time at a coronation.

The Queen now discarded her white garment and received all emblems of sovereignty (the vestments, spurs, jewelled sword, the orb, ring, royal sceptre and the rod of equity and mercy): the supreme moment had arrived. The archbishop, after dedicating the St Edward's Crown at the high altar, moved down the steps to stand before the Queen, sitting in the coronation chair, and gently laid the crown on her head. All princes and princesses, peers and peeresses and kings of arms then shouted, 'God Save the Queen', as they placed their coronets on their heads. Trumpets sounded, bells pealed, and gun salutes were fired from the Tower of London, St James's Park, and other places. The Queen had been crowned.

The Queen was then enthroned, a ceremony which has its origin in Saxon times and which signified that she had taken possession of her realm. She was lifted up into the raised throne by the archbishop, bishops and peers, ready to receive the homage of her subjects, the last act of the coronation.

First the archbishop gave homage, followed by Prince Philip, who knelt at the Queen's feet and placed his hands between hers, swearing, '. . . to become your liege man of life and limb, and of earthly worship and faith and truth I will bear unto you to live and die against all manner of folks. So help me, God'. He rose, mounted the steps of the throne to touch the crown, and kissed the Queen on her left cheek. Her uncle the Duke of Gloucester, her cousin the Duke of Kent, and the senior peers of each degree then similarly paid homage.

The communion service was then resumed. Having laid aside her crown, sceptre and rod, the Queen and her husband, as man and wife, received the Holy Sacrament from the archbishop. After the blessing, the triumphant *Te Deum* was sung. The Queen, with her nobles and bishops, then passed into St Edward's Chapel. When she emerged, a fanfare again blazed out, and the procession passed down the nave to the singing of the National Anthem. In her purple robe, and wearing the lighter Imperial State Crown, the Queen looked dignified and radiantly happy. Still holding the sceptre in her right hand and the orb in her left, she walked between the brilliant ranks of the great assembly towards the west door.

At five minutes to three in the afternoon, the great procession left the Abbey on the long route back to Buckingham Palace, through the West End, past Hyde Park Corner and Marble Arch to Oxford Circus and Piccadilly Circus. It then passed down the Haymarket, through the Admiralty Arch and into the Mall. The rain was intermittent, but the crowd roared a welcome to the 10,000 marching service men and women, giving a special cheer to the Canadian Mounties in their red coats, the 'diggers' from Australia, and Sir Winston Churchill. As the Queen re-entered her coach at the Abbey, the head of the procession had already reached Stanhope Gate in Hyde Park, two miles away.

The Queen of Tonga, well over six feet tall, received an enthusiastic greeting. Travelling with the Sultan of Kelantan,

Far left *Four days after the coronation, the Queen Mother, the Queen and Princess Margaret grip the rail in excitement at the finish of the Coronation Derby.*

Left *The Queen's colt* Auriole *was a fancied runner but finished in second place to* Pinza *ridden by Sir Gordon Richards, seen here being congratulated by Her Majesty and Prince Philip.*

she insisted that their landau should remain open, despite heavy rain. Afterwards she said, 'If the people could wait so long in the rain and cold, I quite willingly faced getting wet myself'. The crowd's excitement reached a peak when the coronation coach passed by, bearing the Queen, still wearing her crown, and Prince Philip. By the time she arrived back to Buckingham Palace, six and a half hours had passed since her departure. Then, accompanied by her family, she mounted to the balcony to take the salute of the fly-past of the Royal Air Force. This was delayed by the rain and low cloud, the pilots keeping an open formation of seven groups, each of twenty-four planes, instead of the planned single compact formation.

Throughout that evening the celebrations continued, and time after time the Queen and Prince Philip were summoned to the balcony by the continual chant, 'We want the Queen!' From the balcony she pressed a button giving the signal for the illuminations – the Mall and other parts of London now sparkled with light. As Big Ben struck midnight the Queen made her final appearance, acknowledging the deafening cheers with a last wave and grateful smile. As the door swung to behind her, this memorable day came to a happy end.

For the remainder of the week crowds continued to gather along the Mall and outside the Palace. The Queen and Prince Philip toured around London and the suburbs, driving in an open car through streets lined by cheering spectators, many of whom were school children, waving their Union Jacks. From time to time the procession slowed up to give hospital patients, watching at their windows, the opportunity of greeting them.

On Saturday 6th June the Queen and Prince Philip went to the Derby where record crowds saw the Queen's horse, *Aureole*, finish in second place to the favourite, ridden by Gordon Richards, who had just been awarded a knighthood in the Coronation Honours. Only a few days later at Ascot the tables were turned. The Queen's horse, *Choir Boy*, beat *Brunetto*, ridden by Gordon Richards, in the Royal Hunt Cup.

On Monday 8th June, the Queen, Prince Philip and the Queen Mother, together with a large party, were present at Covent Garden for a gala performance of *Gloriana*, especially composed for the occasion by Benjamin Britten. The climax of the festival was reached a week after Coronation Day when the couple attended a Service of Thanksgiving at St Paul's Cathedral given by the peoples of the Commonwealth. In June and July the Queen and her husband made their long awaited visits to Scotland, Northern Ireland and Wales, which were followed in October by a tour to New Zealand and Australia.

Post-coronation scenes. The new Queen leaves St Paul's Cathedral (above left) *after the Thanksgiving Service held on 9th June and, during her coronation tour of Great Britain, she is welcomed to a house in Balfour Road, Penilee, Glasgow* (above right) *and receives an excited welcome from young children in the New Kent Road in South London* (right).

FIRST YEARS OF THE NEW REIGN

The Queen and Prince Philip left London Airport on 23rd November 1953 for their first Commonwealth tour which was to take them round the world. They flew out to the West Indies via Gander Airport, Newfoundland, and joined the *Gothic* in Bermuda. This was the first time a reigning sovereign had visited the islands and here and in Jamaica, the next country on their route, the couple received a splendid welcome in sweltering weather. Despite Jamaica's intense heat, in which few people drive in open cars, the Queen and the Prince travelled with the roof down, she under a parasol which she laid aside whenever people in the waiting crowds waved to her.

After the *Gothic* had steamed through the Panama Canal, the couple received a tremendous welcome at Suva, capital of Fiji, where they arrived on 17th December. Here again Elizabeth was the first sovereign to visit the islands since Fiji had been ceded to Queen Victoria in 1874. The chiefs, clad in picturesque native dress, paid homage to the Queen on board the *Gothic*. One chief presented the tabua, or whale's tooth, a prized possession.

Instead of the usual cheering when the party landed on Fijian soil, silence reigned, for this is the traditional Fijian greeting of respect. Even so, a few minutes afterwards a great roar broke out from onlookers, but the Fijians lining the route remained silent as the royal party drove to Albert Park in Suva, where the traditional drink of yaqona (other islands call it kava) was offered in coconut shells. Among those who welcomed the Queen was John Christian, a descendant of Fletcher Christian, the celebrated *Bounty* mutineer, who had come with his wife from Pitcairn Island, 3,500 miles away.

From Fiji the royal party flew to Tonga to renew their friendship with Queen Salote, who had made such an impression on the British people at the Coronation. Salote, smiling and happy, and her Tongan people gave the visitors such a warm reception that the Queen told her, 'No wonder these are called the Friendly Islands'. While in Tonga, the Queen and Prince Philip were shown the very ancient tortoise, since deceased, which had once belonged to Captain Cook.

Two days before Christmas the *Gothic* entered Auckland's Waitemata Harbour, escorted by hundreds of yachts and small craft. The party landed in New Zealand in drizzle, reminiscent of coronation day in London, but this did not dampen their reception. The crowd, waiting drenched outside Auckland's Town Hall, shouted, 'Give her an umbrella,' and Mr Buttle, the Deputy Mayor, handed the Prime Minister, Mr Holland, a plastic raincoat to protect the Queen from the rain. To which the Queen, turning to Mr Buttle, responded, 'Thank you very much, Sir Walter Raleigh'.

The Maoris set aside any resentment which had lingered on since their lands were ceded to the crown by treaty in 1840. At a picturesque ceremony at Waitangi, a descendant of the Maori leader who had chopped down the flagpole as an act of defiance now told Elizabeth that, 'Just as your great ancestress, Queen Victoria, offered us her royal protection, so do we now unfold

left A photograph by Lord Snowdon taken in the Music Room at Buckingham Palace in October 1957.

right Both wearing the mantle and star of the Order of the Thistle, the Queen and Prince Philip leave St Gile's Cathedral, Edinburgh, in June 1953.

ourselves under your mantle of love. We thank God for a century and more of British rule.'

It was from Auckland that the Queen delivered her first Christmas message on radio and television. At its conclusion she made a sorrowful reference to the terrible New Zealand train disaster which had just cast a cloud over the Christmas celebrations. 'I know,' said the Queen, 'there is no one in New Zealand and indeed throughout the Commonwealth, who will not join with my husband and me in sending to those who mourn a message of sympathy in their loss'.

The New Zealand tour included the State Opening of the thirtieth Parliament in Wellington on 12th January 1954, again in pouring rain. Wearing her coronation gown and a diamond tiara, Elizabeth made history. This was the second time only that a monarch had thus officiated in the Southern Hemisphere. (The first time was when her father, King George VI, opened the South African Parliament.) On the following day the Queen held the first Privy Council meeting in New Zealand.

After the royal couple had toured North and South Island, the Prime Minister, Mr Holland, told them, 'It is impossible to calculate the benefits of this remarkable tour. New Zealand has known nothing like it before'. The Queen replied, 'We have enjoyed every minute of our stay . . .' On the last day of January the *Gothic* made a brief detour up the magnificent Milford Sound, one of the most spectacular sights in New Zealand. The next day the Queen received her first Australian welcome when an escorting squadron of the Royal Australian Navy took over escort duty in the Tasman Sea.

On Wednesday 3rd February the *Gothic* steamed into Sydney's majestic harbour, to be welcomed by gaily decorated yachts, launches and speedboats. As the Queen stepped on to Australian soil, a million people stood to welcome her. 'The Queen of Australia comes home at last,' cried one commentator as she stepped ashore. The crowd hushed as the Queen took the microphone to say, 'I have always looked forward to my first visit to this country, but now there is the added satisfaction to me that I am able to meet my Australian people as their Queen. I am proud indeed to be at the head of a nation that has achieved so much'.

The first official act to be carried out was the Queen's laying of a wreath in memory of the thousands of Australians who had fallen in battle alongside their comrades from other Commonwealth countries. That night Sydney put on the greatest firework display the city had ever known, concluding with a pyrotechnic portrait of the Queen some 50 feet square.

During the tour of Australia the royal party travelled as far north as Cairns, Queensland, on the Great Barrier Reef, and as far west as Perth. On 15th February, again in her coronation gown, the Queen opened her first Australian Parliament. Mr Robert Menzies, the Prime Minister, told her at the state banquet, 'You are in your own country, among your own people . . . we are yours, all parties, all creeds. Skilled as you are in the noble arts of Queenship, young though you are in years, may I say this to you: you can count on us.'

On 1st April, after a memorable visit, the Queen and Prince Philip once again boarded the *Gothic* to begin their return journey, bound for the Cocos Islands and Ceylon. Among the ceremonies they watched in Ceylon was a *raja perahera* (royal procession) at the Buddhist Temple of the Tooth. After opening the Ceylon Parliament, the couple sailed across the Indian

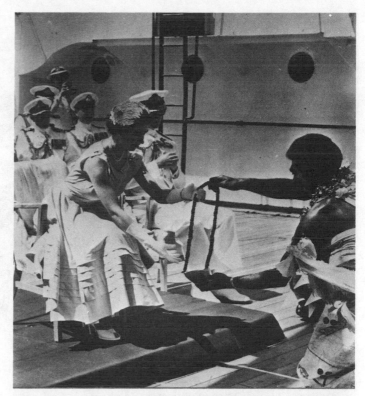

left *In this delightful picture of the new Queen Elizabeth, she chats with Philip at a film premier in October 1953. Princess Margaret is on her left.*

top *On her first Commonwealth tour as sovereign in December 1953 the Queen is welcomed in Fiji by being presented with a Tabua or whale's tooth attached to a plaited cord of sinnet.*

above *On the same tour the royal couple is bid farewell after visiting Queen Salote of Tonga.*

Ocean to Aden, where Philip was fascinated by the great new oil refinery. The party then flew to Entebbe, the airport where the Queen had begun her sad flight home on her father's death. Now she had the duty of opening the sluices of the new Owen Falls Dam on the Nile.

On 1st May, at Tobruk in North Africa, the couple reunited with their children, Prince Charles and Princess Anne, who were on their first visit abroad. They had sailed from Portsmouth in the royal yacht *Britannia* to stay in Malta with their father's uncle and aunt, Lord and Lady Mountbatten, before meeting their parents.

After visiting Malta and Gibraltar on the last lap of their tour, the royal party sailed home aboard *Britannia*, arriving at Westminster Pier, London, on 15th May, having been away for 173 days. It was universally agreed that it had been the most successful royal tour ever undertaken, and it was probably the Queen's most arduous one.

The Queen enjoyed just two free days at home before official business started in earnest on 18th May. That day she presided at a meeting of the Prince's Council of the Duchy of Cornwall, as her son the Duke was a minor; she received two Argentine ministers; and saw Mr David Eccles, the Minister of Works, concerning alterations carried out at Buckingham Palace during her absence.

As well as her series of appointments, undertaken sometimes jointly with Prince Philip, but more often on her own, Elizabeth fulfilled throughout the year the many duties which now take place annually. For example, the Trooping the Colour on her official birthday took place on 10th June, her husband's thirty-third birthday, and she took the salute on her horse *Winston*. The fourteenth of June was Garter Day, when Windsor was *en fête*. This was a special occasion, since Sir Winston Churchill was installed a Knight of the Garter. The colourful procession in robes, velvet mantles and hats plumed with ostrich feathers, passed from the Castle down the hill into St George's Chapel, where the service took place in brilliant sunshine.

On 15th July, for the first time this century, the Lords Lieutenant of counties entertained their sovereign to dinner at Lancaster House, presenting to the Queen a painting by Terence Cuneo of Prince Philip's act of homage at the Coronation.

Nineteen fifty-four was the centenary of the Battle of Balaclava, and 9th October saw the Queen attending celebrations at Stirling Castle given by the Argyll and Sutherland Highlanders. Then, on 26th November, with Prince Philip and the Queen Mother, the Queen went to the Balaclava Ball at the Hyde Park Hotel, London, given by the Hussar and Lancer Regiments who took part in the historic Charge of the Light Brigade. All the officers wore full dress uniforms and the Colonel of the 11th Hussars was dressed in the actual tunic and jacket worn by the Earl of Cardigan, who had led the Charge.

The Queen replies to a Maori welcome (above) *at Waitangi, New Zealand, in January 1954 during the same world tour. She inspected a royal guard provided by the New Zealand Air Force at Bluff on South Island* (right), *and sixty prize merino sheep* (above right) *at an agricultural show at Dubbo in New South Wales, during her visit to Australia.*

Between these events came the state visit of the Emperor of Ethiopia, on whom the Queen bestowed the Order of the Garter. He was no stranger to England, for he had sought refuge here in 1936 when the Italians overran his country, remaining in exile until 1941.

With the impending resignation of Sir Winston Churchill, the Queen dined for the first time with her Prime Minister and Lady Churchill on 4th April 1955 at 10 Downing Street. The following day the departure of this grand old man, who was first elected to Parliament in the reign of Queen Victoria, was announced. Although the identity of his successor was no secret, it was not known officially until eleven o'clock in the morning on 6th April that the Queen had asked Sir Anthony Eden to form a government.

In 1955 the ceremony of distributing the Royal Maundy took place in Southwark Cathedral, which was then celebrating its diocesan golden jubilee. Every Maundy Thursday, the day before Good Friday, the sovereign gives specially minted coins as alms to as many pensioners of each sex as the monarch has years of age. Westminster Abbey had been closed in 1953 for coronation preparations, and so the Maundy Service had been held that year in St Paul's Cathedral. This was so well received that a decision was taken to revert to the earlier practice of distributing Maundy in cathedrals and abbeys throughout England.

On 22nd June the Queen launched on Clydeside the Cana-

dian Pacific liner, the *Empress of Britain*. Later that day, with Prince Philip, she boarded the royal yacht *Britannia* at Rosyth to sail across the North Sea to Norway on her first state visit. Their host was King Haakon VII, an eighty-two year old widower, who was then celebrating his golden jubilee. He and Crown Prince Olaf personally welcomed the couple ashore in Oslo, and at the subsequent banquet the King spoke of the hospitality he had received in Britain during the war when the Germans drove him out of Norway. Unfortunately, only a few days after their visit, he slipped and fractured a thigh, which was only partially healed before his death two years later. After the state visit the Queen and Prince Philip returned to Scotland to carry out engagements in Dundee and Edinburgh, taking up residence in Holyroodhouse.

On 21st October 1955, a day of wind and rain, the Queen unveiled the national memorial statue of her father King George VI in Carlton Gardens, London, saying, 'His fortitude, determination and confidence throughout the perilous autumn of 1940, and the anxious years that followed, were an inspiration to all who loved freedom. He was the living symbol of our steadfastness ... Much was asked of my father in personal sacrifice and endeavour, often in the face of illness; his courage in overcoming it endeared him to everybody. He shirked no task, however difficult, and to the end he never faltered in his duty to his people.'

Plans were made towards the end of 1955 for the Queen's visit to Nigeria, a country then in the throes of independence within the Commonwealth. With this in mind, a Nigerian equerry, Major Aguiyi-Ironso of the Nigerian Regiment, was appointed in December, the first non-white to join the House-

hold since Queen Victoria's unpopular Indian Munchi. In planning the Nigerian tour, details of the only comparable precedent, the Durbar – the elaborate ceremonial at Delhi in 1911 when King George V celebrated his accession as Emperor of India – were of little help, since this historic event really belonged to a bygone age.

The Queen and Prince Philip left London Airport on 27th January 1956, a bitterly cold day, being seen off by a number of Nigerians in national dress. By coincidence the couple travelled on the same plane as had brought them home so suddenly from East Africa after King George VI's death. They received a great welcome in Lagos, and throughout Nigeria there was an extensive round of appointments. At Kaduna they held the Durbar at which 8,000 warriors participated. In one thrilling event, the horsemen of the Jahi tribe charged at tremendous speed across the arena, pulling up only a few yards short of the covered dais where the royal party sat.

None of the ceremonial duties the Queen and Prince Philip carried out impressed the Nigerians as much as the single act of going to visit the leper settlement on the Oji River, tne first ever to be visited by members of the royal family. The Queen and Prince Philip shook hands with leprosy sufferers, a ten-year-old girl and a thirteen-year-old boy. The supervisor of the settlement said, 'The Queen's visit will do more to conquer man's fear and hate of the disease than any other single act I can think of. People all over the world will read that the Queen and the Duke penetrated a leper settlement, and this will convince them as nothing else could that most of their fears of the disease are groundless.' From 1956 the Queen adopted eight leper patients, five from Uganda, one from Tanzania and two

from India. Of these, four were eventually discharged, one
died, and three were able to return home to be treated as out-
patients. LEPRA (British Leprosy Relief Association) later
changed the adoption to an outpatient scheme, which the
Queen and Prince Philip still support.

The last city visited in Nigeria was the old walled city of
Kano, on the edge of the great Sahara Desert. Here turbaned
Moslem horsemen, wearing armour handed down as heir-
looms and believed to date from the Crusades, were their
guards of honour. Leaving the vast country of Nigeria, Africa's
largest in population, the Queen and Prince Philip flew back
to London on 17th February.

On 22nd April the Queen entertained the visiting Russian
leaders Marshal Bulganin and Nikita Khrushchev to tea at
Windsor Castle. The purpose of their visit, officially non-
political, was to tour textile plants, but they were given a cool
reception in Britain. Two days later Earl Attlee, the former
Prime Minister, was honoured with the Order of the Garter.
On 11th May the Queen inaugurated the private, informal
luncheon party at Buckingham Palace. The first guest list included the Bishop of London, the Editor of *The Times*, the
Director General of the Boy Scouts International Bureau, a
banker, a civil servant and two members of her Household. So
successful did these luncheons become that they have been
held at intervals ever since. Four days after the second luncheon
the Queen invited the former King Leopold of the Belgians to
tea at Buckingham Palace. This was their first contact since
the King's rift with Britain over the Belgian capitulation in
1940.

The Queen and Prince Philip sailed on 4th June in the royal
yacht *Britannia* on their state visit to Sweden, to repay the
King's and Queen's stay in London. As Queen Louise is an
aunt of Prince Philip, this was in the nature of a family party.
While in Sweden, they were joined by Princess Margaret to
watch the equestrian events of the Olympics, and saw the
British team gain the gold medal for the three-day event, and
the show-jumping team the bronze medal.

The Suez crisis developed from Egypt's seizure of the canal
on 26th July 1956. The Queen was attending Goodwood races
when a special meeting of the Privy Council was held at
Arundel Castle on 3rd August, where she was staying with the
Duke and Duchess of Norfolk. Here she signed a proclamation
calling out the Army Reserve.

Prince Philip left London Airport on 15th October on the
first stage of his round-the-world journey which took him to
Melbourne to open the Olympic Games, and then on to the
Antarctic. The Queen continued to carry out a crowded programme involving a total of 402 public engagements in 1956.

Nineteen fifty-seven proved to be an even busier year: four
state visits were planned to Portugal, France and Denmark,
plus a projected tour of Canada and the United States. On top
of this the continuing Suez situation resulted in much extra
work and worry. On 8th January, Sir Anthony and Lady Eden
travelled to Sandringham on what proved to be no ordinary
visit by the Prime Minister to his sovereign. Eden gave the
news that his doctors had advised him to resign his office immediately, and the Queen travelled to London the next day
for the formal announcement. There was no rumour of a
resignation until that evening when Sir Anthony left Downing
Street for the Palace. Here an announcement was issued at

seven o'clock. At two o'clock in the afternoon on the following day, 10th January, when Mr Harold Macmillan arrived to see the Queen, the waiting crowds knew that he was to be the Prime Minister, and not Mr R. A. Butler as had been expected.

On 11th February the Queen travelled to Lisbon for her four-day state visit to Portugal, where she rejoined Prince Philip after his long tour. Both had endured unkind newspaper reports originating from an American newspaper, which suggested disharmony between the couple. This was promptly denied by Buckingham Palace—the speculation had arisen merely from the circumstances of a lengthy absence. The couple went ashore from *Britannia* in the green and gold Portuguese state barge, which had been used only once since the Queen's great-grandfather King Edward VII had landed in 1903 on a visit to King Carlos. The Queen and Prince Philip, happy to be reunited, received a spontaneous welcome from the Portuguese people, and at one point were showered in rose petals and confetti.

Less than a month afterwards, on 8th April, the Queen and her husband flew to Paris on a state visit to President Coty of France, which proved the most glittering occasion that city had known since the war. (It was the Queen's second visit, for she had been in 1948 as Princess Elizabeth.) Here the Queen showed the world she was an attractive woman. She had a new hairstyle, and her breathtaking dresses by Hartnell vied with

those of leading French couturiers. When the couple appeared on the floodlit balcony of the Opera it was estimated that the crowd below, which stretched as far back as the Louvre, numbered half a million.

As a highlight of the stay in Paris, the royal guests were taken by launch along the Seine to watch a spectacular illuminated river pageant of Parisian history, ending in a firework display. The Queen was particularly impressed when, as the party passed under the bridges of the Seine, 200 boys, the Petits Chanteurs à la Croix de Bois, chanted a medieval hymn, *Pont au Double*. Later when the President decorated Prince Philip with the Legion of Honour, he turned to the Queen, bowed, and said, 'Et maintenant, Madame, l'accolade', inviting her to kiss her husband.

As well as seeing the glories of Paris and the Palace of Versailles, the royal visitors toured Lille and other towns of the industrial north, everywhere receiving a great reception.

The following month, on 21st May, after touring Hull, the Queen and Prince Philip were off again in the royal yacht *Britannia* to make their third state visit of 1957, this time to the King and Queen of Denmark. King Frederik IX, a great exponent of physical culture who went in for strenuous weightlifting exercises, had just strained his back and was in agony. Even so, both visitors and hosts thoroughly enjoyed the visit, and their cheerfulness was echoed by their reception from the

left *In April 1954, the Queen arrives in state to open the Ceylon Parliament. She is welcomed here by the Prime Minister, Sir John Kotalawala.*

above and right *On the homeward Mediterranean leg of her first Commonwealth tour the Queen was triumphantly welcomed in Malta in May.*

left *After dining with her Prime Minister, Sir Winston Churchill, at 10 Downing Street shortly before his resignation, the Queen is shown to her car by her host a little before midnight on 4th April 1955.*

below *The Queen is seen here with Prince Philip, both carrying posies, leaving Southwark Cathedral after the Maundy Service in April 1955.*

right *The Captain General of the Honourable Artillery Company, H M The Queen, inspects pikemen and musketeers at the Artillery Ground, City of London, in July 1955. She presented the HAC with new colours and a warrant of official recognition to the Company of Pikemen and Musketeers.*

Danish people. The informality of this little Scandinavian kingdom strongly contrasted with the recent magnificence of Paris. From Denmark they sailed to Scotland to review the Home Fleet on 27th May at Invergordon.

That summer, in the midst of such a busy year, the Queen was subjected to a series of verbal onslaughts. Previously, the Lord's Day Observance Society, and the League of Cruel Sports, had attacked her and her family. Now the former Lord Altrincham, playwright John Osborne, Malcolm Muggeridge, former Editor of Punch, and others, all joined in to criticize, despite the fact that the Queen is unable to defend herself. The vast majority of her subjects regarded these criticisms as being not only very unfair, but also quite unwarranted.

After a holiday at Balmoral, the Queen and Prince Philip left on 12th October for their tour of Canada and the United States. Although of short duration, five days in Canada and six in the United States, the tour was of such high pressure that on average they were able to sleep only six hours a night. It was then six years since Prince Philip had first taken his wife, then the Princess Elizabeth, to Canada. Now she was present as Queen of Canada for the first time. Wearing her coronation dress to open Parliament, as in the other Commonwealth countries on her world tour, she repeated the words of Queen Elizabeth I, 'Though God hath raised me high, yet this I count the glory of my crown—that I have reigned with your loves'. She concluded by saying, 'Now here in the New World I say to you that it is my wish that in the years before me I may so reign in Canada and be so remembered'. There had been last-minute behind-the-scene difficulties. Barely five minutes before the Queen's arrival the powerful film lights blew all the fuses in the Houses of Parliament, which were repaired only a few seconds before the carriage drew up. The Queen's first solo television appearance was made with great assurance and belied any criticism from Britain that she read all her speeches.

The Canadian tour was a great triumph, blending formality with informality. One morning Philip got up before dawn to go duck-shooting before attending a diplomatic reception, where he told the guests that he had bagged the official limit of eight birds. After a government reception on 15th October the couple shook hands with 1,300 guests in ninety minutes, and then enjoyed a small dinner at the home of the Prime Minister, Mr John Diefenbaker.

The Canadian government and people were particularly pleased that Elizabeth flew to the United States on 14th October as Queen of Canada. At Williamsburg, Virginia, she was presented with a copy of a picture of her American ancestor (through the Queen Mother), Colonel Augustine Warner. At a dinner speech she amused her audience with her references to her ancestor King George III's loss of his American colonies as a result of the War of Independence. 'I am told there is a county in Virginia named for every English King and Queen from Elizabeth I to George III,' she told them, adding, for emphasis, '*even* George III'.

At Jamestown, also in Virginia, the Queen and her husband attended the 350th anniversary of the first British Settlement by a guard of honour dressed in Elizabethan costumes and wearing long curly wigs.

President Eisenhower was waiting at Washington Airport to meet his royal guests. There were nine engagements for the first afternoon and evening. Next day there were fourteen, and the day following thirteen, including watching an American

football match between the Universities of Maryland (the Terrapins) and North Carolina (the Tar-heels). Later the party boarded a train for New York, where the Queen received a standing ovation on addressing the United Nations Assembly. The couple received the traditional New York ticker-tape welcome with huge banners in evidence proclaiming 'Welcome Phil and Liz', lunches with 1500 people and dinner at the Waldorf with 4,000. A policeman on Broadway summed up their great welcome by his comment that, 'I think she's real fine, and anyone who can go through what she is going through is OK in my book'.

In 1958 the Queen suffered acutely from a series of colds, one after another. The first occurred at Sandringham soon after Christmas; the next at Windsor in April, and again during the summer at Balmoral. Some of her engagements had to be cancelled, such as a dinner for her Ascot house party and the Football Association Cup Final, but she insisted on taking the salute at the annual Trooping the Colour in pouring rain. Then, during a tour of Scotland and North East England, she was taken ill on the royal train. Philip persuaded her to return to London immediately while he carried on with various engagements. When he got back to her he found her ill in bed. The sinus trouble from which she was suffering made it impossible for her to travel to the Principality in person to declare her son the Prince of Wales, to her great disappointment.

Ill health did not prevent her, however, from making a state visit with Prince Philip to the Netherlands from 25th to 27th March, the first to that country in our history. She gave Queen Juliana the highly prized honour of the Order of the Garter, which King George VI had given to Queen Wilhelmina in 1944 during her exile in Britain. There has only been one other instance of this premier order of chivalry being conferred upon a mother and daughter—the Queen and the Queen Mother both being Ladies of the Garter. A display of early tulips greeted the visitors, and the royal party toured a diamond

factory in Amsterdam. Here the Queen's invaluable Cullinan diamond which, on this occasion, she wore as a brooch, was greatly admired. As the owner of several Rembrandts, the Queen was particularly pleased to be able to see his paintings and other treasures at the Rijksmuseum. Philip, on the other hand, together with his fellow consort and host, Prince Bernhard, managed to fit in a trial run in the latter's new Ferrari.

During the year foreign heads of state also came to London with all the trappings of ceremony surrounding state visits to the Queen. On 13th May President Cronchi of Italy and his wife arrived at Victoria Station on a three-day visit. Then, on 12th October, Dr Theodor Heuss, President of the German Federal Republic, arrived at Gatwick Airport. He was the first German head of state to have come on an official visit since 1907, when the bellicose Kaiser Wilhelm II had stayed with his uncle King Edward VII. Dr Heuss, an elderly man of high academic standing, brought £5,000 from the German people as a gift towards restoring Coventry Cathedral, a gesture which was much appreciated. He nevertheless received a silent welcome from onlookers unable to forget the war which had ended only thirteen years earlier.

Two days before Dr Heuss arrived, the Queen and Prince Philip, Princess Margaret and the Duke and Duchess of Gloucester were present at St Clement Danes in the Strand, London, when this church, famous for 'the bells of St Clement's' was reconsecrated by the Bishop of London as the Royal Air Force Memorial Church, having been seriously damaged in the war.

On 28th October the Queen opened Parliament in state at Westminster. Though an annual event, this particular occasion had a special significance, for the 1958 opening was the first to be televised. When the Prime Minister announced this, *The Times* recorded that the news was received with a 'rather thoughtful cheer' reflecting the caution with which members viewed this innovation. Although the procession in the Irish State Coach from Buckingham Palace to Westminster is a customary sight, the ceremony inside Parliament had hitherto been witnessed only by a privileged few. Now the Queen, wearing her magnificent robe of state and the Imperial State Crown, was watched by the world as she delivered her speech.

Prince Philip left in January 1959 on a round-the-world 100-day tour which took him to India, where he visited the Taj Mahal, Pakistan, the Far East and the Pacific, returning at the end of April in time to join the Queen in welcoming the Shah of Iran on his state visit, beginning on 5th May. By this time, the plans for the forthcoming tour of Canada were well on the way. This was to be the most extensive visit to Canada the Queen had yet undertaken – in all 16,000 miles, and with forty-five overnight stops. When someone commented on this heavy programme the Queen replied, 'I'm not going on holiday but to work'.

The Queen and her husband flew out on 18th June to Newfoundland, where she opened the new air terminal at Gander. From here they sailed in the royal yacht *Britannia* to Quebec City. Canada was baking that summer. Montreal was sweltering in the nineties, and the Queen undertook a fourteen-hour programme in this intense heat in Toronto. She confided in the Prime Minister, Mr Diefenbaker, that she was expecting

left *Jahi horsemen raise their swords to salute the Queen during the Durbar, held at Kaduna, Nigeria, during the royal visit in February 1956.*

right *In Lagos, the Queen was welcomed by Chief Oba-Adeniji-Adele II in the welcome shade of a beautifully ornate parasol.*

below *In contrast weather-wise, back home in the Western Islands of Scotland in August 1956, shelter is provided by a standard British umbrella as the Queen inspects a guard of honour by 8th Argyll and Sutherland Highlanders at Oban.*

Above and left *The state visit to France in April 1957 was the most glittering occasion the country had known since the dark days of war and occupation. At Lille (above), excited crowds rush forward to catch a glimpse of the Queen and at the Elysée Palace (left) she is entertained by President Coty at a magnificent state banquet.*

right *On the highly successful Canadian royal tour of October 1957, the Queen and Prince Philip pause at the head of the steps of the Peace Tower, Ottawa, while the royal salute is played.*

her third child, but would not hear of curtailing her tour. At Quebec the couple met President and Mrs Eisenhower at the airport, for one of the main purposes of the visit was the joint opening of the great St Lawrence Seaway. This Canadian-American venture, which took four-and-a-half years to construct, directly linked the Canadian lakes with world trade. After the ceremonial opening, by the Queen of Canada and the President of the United States, the two stood together on the bridge of the *Britannia* and sailed up the Seaway. Later the Queen crossed the American border to visit the Moses-Sanders Power Dam at Massena, seventy feet above the Seaway, to unveil the International Friendship Monument.

left *In clean white overalls, the Queen made her first coal mine descent at Kirkcaldy, Scotland, in July 1958.*

below *The Queen alights from the royal train at Banff, Alberta, on her 1959 Canadian tour.*

previous page *A magnificently caparisoned elephant provides an impressive mount for the Queen at Benares in February 1961, during her tour of India and Pakistan.*

right *Accompanied by traditional Swiss Guards wearing breast plates and bearing pikes, the royal couple leave the Vatican after an audience with Pope John XXIII in May 1961, the first granted to a British sovereign.*

below *The Queen is entertained in Brussels by King Baudouin and Queen Fabiola during her state visit to Belgium in May 1966. The king sits to the right of the Queen.*

The Queen, with Prince Philip and the Canadian Prime Minister, cruised in the royal yacht down Lake Michigan to Chicago, being the first reigning sovereign ever to have visited that great American city. The couple spent thirteen hours in Chicago, during which they saw the International Fair before returning to Canada. On 10th July, after a busy programme, they travelled by train through the Rockies, and spent a quiet weekend at a private fishing camp by Pennask Lake in British Columbia.

The mid-July programmes in Vancouver and Victoria were exacting—so much so that when the Queen arrived at Whitehorse in Yukon she was near to fainting, and was compelled to cancel her engagements for the day, leaving Philip to undertake them alone. On 20th July she flew direct to Edmonton, while Philip carried on the northern tour as arranged, by going to Yellowknife. The Canadian press attaché, Esmond Butler, not informed of the Queen's pregnancy, stated, 'The Queen was suffering from a stomach upset and from fatigue. She will not be going to Dawson City and will stay indoors today. Prince Philip is going to church alone, and will go to Dawson City . . .' Philip much regretted that the Queen's tour of the north-western territories, his own idea, had to be abandoned. After travelling to the eastern provinces of New Brunswick, Prince Edward Island and Nova Scotia, the couple left for London by air instead of returning by their yacht as had been arranged. Despite the state of the Queen's health the tour was extremely successful, and the Prime Minister, in his farewell speech, said, 'She has seen Canada as few have seen it'. The Queen and Prince Philip arrived at London Airport on the 1st August, and four days later travelled up to Balmoral. On the 7th it was announced that the Queen was expecting a baby early in the new year, and a private secretary flew out to Ghana to inform Dr Nkrumah that, because of the Queen's condition, the royal visit planned for November would have to be postponed.

On 27th August President Eisenhower arrived at London Airport on a five-day visit for talks with Mr Harold Macmillan, the Prime Minister, before meeting Mr Khrushchev, whom he he had invited to the White House. The next day Mr Eisenhower flew to Scotland for a brief holiday at Balmoral. The Queen drove him, his son and his personal physician round the district in her shooting brake. They picnicked outside a summer house on the shore of a loch, and on the following day the President flew back to join the Prime Minister, before going to see President de Gaulle and other European leaders.

At Balmoral the Queen rested as much as possible during that summer. Her medical adviser, Lord Evans, reported that, 'The Queen is in the best of health'. She gave up riding, but walked more than usual, and when she returned to Buckingham Palace she walked each afternoon in the garden. The Queen and Prince Philip eagerly looked forward to the birth of their child.

left *As their colonel-in-chief, the Queen attends the Irish Guards' garden party at Buckingham Palace in June 1966.*

above right *Red Indian chiefs chat with the Queen at Calgary during the 1959 Canadian tour.*

right *The arrival of President Eisenhower as guest of the Queen at Balmoral in August 1959.*

EVENTS
OF THE SIXTIES

The Queen and Prince Philip decided that their third child should be born in the Belgian suite of Buckingham Palace, which is usually allotted to visiting heads of state. The suite was prepared and was ready for over a week, and then on Friday 19th February 1960, in the main bedroom overlooking the gardens, Prince Andrew was born, the first child to be born to a reigning sovereign since 1857, when Queen Victoria gave birth to her ninth and last child, Princess Beatrice. Congratulations to the happy parents flooded into the Palace from all parts of the world.

Three days before the Prince's christening, President and Madame de Gaulle came to Britain on a state visit and were met at the airport by the Duchess of Kent. The Queen was at Victoria Station to meet the party, making her first public appearance since the birth. A firework display was held in St James's Park in honour of the visitors. There is a story that the President asked that the Prince should be given a French name. 'We called our first son Charles,' the Queen is said to have replied, 'and we shall call our second by a French name, Andre,' both these being the President's names. The baby was christened Andrew, after Prince Philip's father, at Buckingham Palace on the 8th April, the day the de Gaulles flew back to France.

Princess Margaret, whose engagement was announced to Antony Armstrong-Jones, the noted photographer, a week after Prince Andrew's birth, was married on 6th May in Westminster Abbey, with the Queen and all members of the royal family present. The Queen lent her sister and brother-in-law the royal yacht *Britannia* for their honeymoon cruise in the Caribbean.

Among the Queen's many engagements that summer was the tercentenary of the Royal Society, held at the Royal Albert Hall in London on 10th July, to which came guests from forty-seven countries, including the Soviet Union and Communist China. Nine days later the King and Queen of Thailand came to London on a state visit. Then, on 5th August, the Queen went to Cardiff for the National Eisteddfod, where she was met by Philip, who sailed from Cowes in *Britannia*. On the following day the couple went to a special service of thanksgiving at Llandaff Cathedral, which had been restored after extensive wartime bomb damage. Elizabeth paid a second informal visit to the Eisteddfod, taking her elder children, Prince Charles

and Princess Anne, before they sailed north to the Shetlands, where the Queen opened the harbour extension. The Shetlands are proud of their Norse heritage, and the last sovereign known to have visited their Islands was King Haakon IV of Norway, in 1263. From Shetland the Queen and her family sailed to Fair Isle and the Orkneys before they disembarked at Aberdeen to carry out engagements there, before driving to Balmoral.

That month the Queen and Philip visited the King and Queen of Denmark. On their return flight on 25th August, when twenty miles out to sea from the Dutch coast, and at a height of 30,000 feet, their Comet aircraft was closely approached by two Sabre jet fighters of the German Air Force. The co-pilot of the Comet later said the planes had iron crosses underneath the wings, and turned in as a pair, passing only about fifty feet above the royal flight. 'It was a very nasty moment,' he said.

On 10th October the Queen and Prince Philip opened the Tay Bridge at Perth, before taking up residence at Holyroodhouse, Edinburgh. At Edinburgh the Queen addressed a special session of the General Assembly of the Church of Scotland, held to celebrate the 400th anniversary of the Reformation in Scotland – the first time a sovereign had been present since 1602. The Queen and Philip then came back to London for the King and Queen of Nepal's state visit.

Early in 1961 the Queen and her husband were to make their long projected visit to India and Pakistan. A special flag was designed for flying in these republics within the Commonwealth, for as they both had their own heads of state,

left *The royal visit to India in January 1961.*

right *President de Gaulle arrives at the Royal Opera House, London, during his state visit in April 1960.*

the Royal Standard would have been inappropriate. The flag created is of gold and blue with a gold fringe, with the Queen's initial 'E' and a royal crown surrounded by a chaplet of roses. Elizabeth was sorry to miss Prince Andrew's first birthday, but Philip was able to show her some of the splendid sights he had already seen, such as the Taj Mahal. On 20th January they were seen off at London Airport by the Queen Mother, Princess Margaret and her husband. At their first stop in Cyprus, the couple had a twenty-minute talk with the new President, Archbishop Makarios. This was the first time an English sovereign had set foot on the island since 1191, when King Richard Coeur de Lion came on his way to the Third Crusade. The party landed at Palam Airport in India on 21st January and were met by the President, Dr Rajendra Prasad, who took them to his residence at New Delhi. Their first engagement was to lay a wreath on Mahatma Gandhi's monument. The President spoke of the influence of Gandhi, 'Who taught us never to acquire an exclusive character'. In that spirit, India's continuing membership of the Commonwealth is an example to the world. From Delhi the royal party went to Jaipur, where Philip witnessed a tiger hunt, before returning to the capital for the Republic Day celebrations.

In Pakistan the Queen reviewed the fleet in Karachi Harbour. The couple then drove to the Khyber Pass on the North-West Frontier before flying on to Dacca, then in East Pakistan, but now the capital of Bangladesh. They crossed the Himalayas within a mile of the world's highest peak, Mount Everest, to pay state visits to the King of Nepal and the Shah of Iran.

On their return trip the couple paid a state visit to President and Signora Gronchi of Italy, arriving on 1st May. At Vatican City, Pope John XXIII received the Queen for an audience of twenty-five minutes, the first ever given to a British sovereign. While in Italy the royal party toured Naples, Rome, Venice, Florence, Milan and Turin. They had privately visited Rome ten years earlier, when staying with Philip's cousin, Queen Helen of Roumania, at her villa near Florence, and she was in Rome to welcome them again. The couple arrived home from their eastern tour on 9th May.

There was a family wedding on 8th June, when the Queen's cousin, the Duke of Kent, married Katharine Worsley of Hovingham Hall, Yorkshire. Appropriately enough, the ceremony took place in York Minster. The last royal wedding there had been in 1328, when Edward III had married Philippa of Hainault. Many members of the European royal families who gathered for the ceremony were invited by the Queen to a birthday ball for her husband given at Buckingham Palace two days later.

On 8th August the Queen and Philip visited Northern Ireland. They landed from the royal yacht *Britannia* at Carrig-fergus and drove to Belfast. The next day they toured the shipyard of Harland & Wolff, and Philip sailed his yacht *Coweslip* at the Royal Ulster Yacht Club Regatta. From Bangor the couple sailed to Scotland.

On 9th November the royal party left London for their West African tour, and spent their fourteenth wedding anniversary in Ghana. Here they saw durbars of chiefs, the site of the dam for the Volta River Project, and fulfilled many other engagements before leaving on 20th for Liberia, where they lunched with President and Mrs Tubman. From here they went to Sierra Leone, where they attended a service in St George's Cathedral, Freetown, the oldest in West Africa, and thence on to the Gambia. From the Gambian capital Bathurst, Philip piloted his own aircraft, a Heron of the Queen's flight, to Dar-es-Salaam in Tanganyika to attend the independence celebrations. His 4,500-mile flight across central Africa drew some criticism from those concerned with his safety. The route across jungles, swamps and deserts carefully skirted the Congo war zone, and Philip pointed out not only that he would have a co-pilot, but also that the journey would be undertaken in three easy stages. Even so, the Queen arranged for three aircraft, seventy miles apart, to maintain radio contact with the Prince for the duration of the flight. Meanwhile the Queen returned

from Bathurst to London.

During much of the early part of 1962, Philip was away touring South America. Then, after flying Prince Charles to Gordonstoun for the beginning of his first term at the school, he joined the Queen in the Netherlands in May for the silver wedding celebrations of Queen Juliana and Prince Bernhard.

On 25th May the Queen, with the Archbishops of Canterbury and York, was present when the new Coventry Cathedral was reconsecrated by its Bishop, Dr Bardsley. The new cathedral, attached to the ruins of the old which had been blitzed in the war, was designed by Sir Basil Spence, cost one-and-a-half million pounds to build, and took seven years to complete. Vast crowds came, and still come, to see this great feat of modern architecture, which contains Epstein's sculpture of St Michael and the Devil, and, behind the High Altar, Graham

Sutherland's masterpiece, his tapestry of Christ in majesty, the biggest in the world.

On 9th July the Queen attended the masque by John Betjeman, with music by Raymond Leppard, at the Mansion House. This formed part of the celebrations of the Festival of London, and on the following day she welcomed the President of Liberia and Mrs Tubman on their state visit. A week later the royal couple left on their Sussex tour, during which they visited the Regency exhibition at Brighton.

The Commonwealth nations subscribed to erect the new building of the Commonwealth Institute in Kensington High Street, London, which the Queen opened on 6th November, with the High Commissioners of each Commonwealth country in attendance. Elizabeth said, 'It is the thread of personal concern and understanding between individual people that

weaves a strong fabric of the modern Commonwealth'.

At the beginning of February 1963, the Queen and Prince Philip flew off on a tour of Fiji, New Zealand and Australia. The couple arrived at the Bay of Islands, New Zealand, on 6th February 1963 for the 123rd anniversary of the signing of the Treaty of Waitangi. They later sailed in the royal yacht *Britannia* for Auckland and the east coast towns of Napier and Hawkes Bay, before arriving at Wellington to open Parliament and hold the official meeting of the Privy Council.

At Wellington the Queen presented to St Paul's Cathedral the silver chalice and paten used by her grandparents on their 1901 tour, and established the Queen Elizabeth II National Arts Council and the Post Graduate Fellowship, which provides annual fellowship under the administration of the Maori Foundation.

above *On Valentine's Day in Dacca, East Pakistan (now Bangladesh), a little girl in local costume presents a bouquet to the Queen during a reception given to her by the citizens of Dacca.*

left *The Queen is welcomed at Palam Airport, New Delhi, on 21st January 1961, at the start of her six-week tour of India and Pakistan. President Prasad stands between the Queen and Prince Philip and Mr Nehru and Mrs Pandit appear on the right.*

The royal party sailed to Nelson for Prince Philip to visit the Outward Bound School and, after visiting Dunedin and Christchurch in South Island, they left by air on 18th February for Canberra.

The visit to Australia coincided with the fiftieth anniversary celebrations of the founding and naming of Canberra as the capital city, and the main ceremony was held at Park Place facing Parliament House. The Queen then said, 'Half a century ago Canberra was little more than a dream in the minds of a few men. Today it is an established and flourishing city, growing daily in national and international stature. Few nations are given the chance to plan and build their capital from the very beginning. Fifty years ago there were many to say that it was a ridiculous idea, and even today critical comment is not altogether unheard of in some of the older cities. Yet Australia, with a population of little more than a half what it is today, grasped the opportunity with both hands . . .'

The Queen and Prince Philip visited the Australian state capitals and the Snowy Mountains Hydro-electric Scheme, the biggest project of its kind in Australia, which covers 3,000 square miles on the south-east corner of New South Wales. They went to Alice Springs, the Queen's first visit to the outback, where she talked to the people over the Flying Doctor radio network. From here the couple toured the Northern Territory, in whose capital, Darwin, they watched tribal dances by the Aborigines and attended a rodeo. From Darwin they sailed westwards to Perth in the royal yacht *Britannia*, and on 27th March left Sydney Airport to fly back to Britain.

Three weeks after their return, royal guests from Europe began to arrive to attend the wedding of the Queen's cousin, Princess Alexandra of Kent, to Mr Angus Ogilvy, second son of the Earl of Airlie, head of an historic Scottish family. On 22nd April, the day following her thirty-seventh birthday, the

Queen entertained the couple at Windsor Castle, where the state apartments had just been restored to their earlier magnificence. The guests included the King of Norway, the Queens of Denmark, Sweden and Greece, and two former Queens, Victoria Eugenie of Spain and Helen of Roumania. After a dinner party for nearly 100 guests, the ball which followed was the largest to have taken place at Windsor for more than a century, with 1,600 people attending. Prince Charles and Princess Anne, though not at the dinner-party, paid a short visit to the ball, during which the fourteen-year-old Prince danced with his cousin Princess Clarissa of Hesse. Then, on 24th April, the Queen and other members of the royal family attended the royal wedding in Westminster Abbey.

Harold Macmillan was taken ill that autumn, and on 18th October he resigned office as Prime Minister. That day the Queen visited him in the King Edward VII hospital for Officers in London. Later it was announced that she had received the Earl of Home to invite him to form a government, and on the day following he came to the Palace to kiss hands as Prime Minister. He took advantage of the terms of the peerage act, passed that year, to disclaim his Scottish titles, for today it would hardly be possible for a peer to take office. As a Knight of the Thistle, henceforward he was known as Sir Alec Douglas-Home, until he received a life peerage in 1974.

On 22nd November the world received the shattering news that John Fitzgerald Kennedy, President of the United States, had been assassinated while travelling in an open car through Dallas, Texas. Prince Philip flew to attend his funeral in Washington, and on 1st December the Queen and the Queen Mother attended a memorial service in St George's Chapel, Windsor.

At the New Year celebrations for 1964 at Sandringham, the Queen was one of the four enceinte royal ladies present, leaving only the Queen Mother and Princess Marina, Duchess of Kent, available in London to carry out royal duties. Arrangements had already been made in February for the Queen Mother to leave for New Zealand and Australia, although an operation for appendicitis postponed her visit.

Prince Edward was born at Buckingham Palace on 10th March 1964, to the great happiness of his parents. The following day, though Philip was unwilling to leave so soon after the birth, he had to represent the Queen at the funeral of King Paul of the Hellenes. With Princess Marina, Duchess of Kent, he left for Athens. King Paul and Queen Frederika had visited London only eight months earlier. The wedding of their son, now King Constantine, was already fixed for June, and it was decided that it should not be postponed.

On 5th October the Queen and Prince Philip left for Canada to cover the path taken by the Fathers of Confederation, who went from Prince Edward Island to the city of Quebec in 1864 during the preliminary negotiations leading to the Confederation in 1867. They received a good welcome in Prince Edward Island, but in the French-Canadian city of Quebec they drove through almost empty streets. Many French-Canadians advocate a separatist policy through secession from the Dominion of Canada, and as there had been noisy demonstrations of students, the royal couple were prepared for a cool reception. 'There's no need to worry,' the Queen told her staff, 'I'll be as safe as houses'. Her speech to the Canadian legislature, in which she referred to the possibility of bringing the Canadian Constitution up to date, was well received. After the tension in Quebec, Ottawa, which they visited on Thanksgiving Day, gave them a warm welcome. The Queen returned home alone while Prince Philip travelled on to the Bahamas and Mexico.

In October, as a result of the Conservative Party's defeat in the General Election, the Queen invited Harold Wilson, Leader of the Labour Party, to form an administration to

above *The royal yacht* Britannia *is seen here moored for Cowes week in July and August 1961.*

left *During the royal visit to Port Loko, Sierra Leone, in November 1961, the Queen and Prince Philip put their heads together to discuss the traditionally bare-bosomed Susu dancers.*

right *The Mayor of Picton, New Zealand, escorts the Queen past another enthusiastic welcome from school children during her twelve-day tour in February 1963.*

replace that of Sir Alec Douglas-Home.

That Christmas, with so many young children in the royal family, the traditional Christmas party at Sandringham was switched to Windsor where there was more room. The party then left for Norfolk for the new year celebrations.

Sir Winston Churchill died at the age of ninety on 24th January 1965 at his London home in Hyde Park Gate, and was given the first state funeral of a non-royal subject since that of the great Duke of Wellington in 1852. He lay in state for three days in Westminster Hall, where the Queen, Prince Philip, Princess Margaret and the Lord Snowdon, paid their respects. The Queen, Prince Philip, and Queen Mother and the Prince of Wales were among the members of the royal family who attended the state funeral in St Paul's Cathedral, as did many heads of state, members of foreign royal families and distinguished visitors, including the Kings of the Belgians, Denmark, Norway and Greece, the Queen of the Netherlands, the Grand Duke of Luxembourg, President de Gaulle and General Eisenhower.

On 1st February the Queen and Prince Philip flew to Africa

left and right *On the same trip but this time in Australia in March 1963, the Queen is welcomed by children in the Northern Territory between Alice Springs and Darwin* (left), *and by children plus a dog at Geraldton, Western Australia* (right).

below *On the east lawn at Windsor Castle in June 1964, the Queen inspects battalions of the Coldstream Guards after presenting them with their new colours.*

on a state visit to Ethiopia, arriving at Addis Ababa. The elderly Emperor Haile Selassie showed them many sights including the Blue Nile Falls, and took them on horseback to a picnic at Menegasha Woods, fifteen miles from the capital, to taste Ethiopian food. Nine days later they flew to Khartoum to pay a state visit to Sudan, then in a state of political uncertainty after the downfall of the military regime. There was a truce during the royal visit, and the Queen was assured she would be in no danger. After spending the night in the Sudan, the couple flew back to Ethiopia to resume the royal tour, before returning to London.

The Queen met the Duchess of Windsor for the first time since her accession at the London Clinic, when she went there on 15th March to visit her uncle the Duke, then aged seventy, who had undergone three operations on his left eye. She drove up in the early evening, and talked to the couple for twenty-five minutes. The Duke in his dressing gown and pyjamas, had his eye bandaged but rose to greet her.

On 18th May the Queen and Prince Philip went on a state visit to the Federal Republic of Germany, a trip which had been arranged earlier but had been postponed owing to Prince Edward's birth. The old enmity between the two nations was finally healed when a British sovereign set foot on German soil for the first time for fifty-two years. The couple had a full programme during which they visited several cities, all of which gave them a great welcome, including Bonn, where they stayed for two days, Munich, Stuttgart, Cologne and Dusseldorf. They made a brief visit to West Berlin, and also visited Hanover and Hamburg.

After a day of ceremonies at the Bavarian capital, Munich, they attended a three-hour gala performance of Richard Strauss's 'Der Rosenkavalier' at the State Opera House. From here they paid a private weekend visit to the large castle, Schloss Salem, of Philip's sister Princess Sophie and her husband Prince George of Hanover. After their train journey they alighted at Salem Station, specially opened after a ten-year closure and made the last stage of the journey to the Schloss a picturesque one in an ancient open carriage. Also waiting to greet them were Philip's mother Princess Alice, then aged eighty, and his other sisters, both widowed: Princess Theodora

who also lives at Salem, and Princess Margarita of Hohenlohe-Langenburg, together with several younger relations. Philip delighted the Queen by showing her the part of the Schloss which had once been his school, including the old desk where he had cut his initials.

The party embarked at Hamburg in the royal yacht *Britannia*, having made a major contribution towards improving Anglo-German relations. It was typical of the Queen's greeting in the Federal Republic that a newspaper headlined, 'Your Majesty, Germany belongs to you'. Their progress achieved far more in the cause of friendship, and therefore peace, than all the political speeches uttered since the war. There was the added practical result, dear to Philip, that the youth scheme between Britain and West Germany was extended.

That summer, on 19th September, the Queen and other members of the royal family attended a service of thanksgiving at Westminster Abbey for the twenty-fifth anniversary of the Battle of Britain, after which Elizabeth unveiled a memorial stone to Sir Winston Churchill. She then watched a fly-past of Lightning aircraft of Fighter Command before returning to Balmoral.

The Queen took part in the 700th celebrations of the Duchy of Lancaster, on 27th October, by attending a special service in the Queen's Chapel of the Savoy, London, with a congregation of about 200 people connected with the Duchy. As is customary on these occasions, the congregation sang the National Anthem beginning thus:

> 'God Save our Gracious Queen
> Long Live our Noble Duke . . .'

The evening reception was held at St James's Palace for about 700 of those connected with the Duchy, including farmers and their wives. The toast in Lancashire was traditionally 'The Queen, Duke of Lancaster', but since the recent boundary changes it has been changed to 'The Queen, Duke of the North West'.

above *Another review, this time of the Royal Marines in ski uniform, the highlight of celebrations for the Corps' tercentenary in July 1964.*
right *Distinguished royal guests, heads of state and politicians leave St Paul's Cathedral after the state funeral of Sir Winston Churchill in January 1965.*

above *Emperor Haile Selassie shows the Queen the impressive Tississat Falls on the Blue Nile, during the state visit to Ethiopia in February 1965.*

left *Mrs Kennedy and her children, Caroline and John, join the Queen at the inauguration service of the Kennedy Memorial Stone at Runnymede on 14th May 1965. Standing between the Queen and Prince Philip are Lord Harlech, formerly Ambassador to the USA, and the Kennedys. Behind are Princess Lee Radziwill, Mrs Kennedy's sister, and Robert and Edward Kennedy and their wives.*

right *Presentation of new colours to the Hussars in Ottawa took place during the royal visit to Canada in July 1967.*

left *Leaving St Paul's Cathedral after the annual service of the Most Distinguished Order of St Michael and St George in July 1968, the Queen as Sovereign of the Order displays the Star and Mantle of Saxon blue satin lined with scarlet silk.*

above *Patriotic welcome for the Queen during her visit to the Seychelles Islands in March 1972.*

right *Something of the peaceful, relaxing atmosphere of Balmoral is captured in this photograph by Patrick Lichfield, taken in October 1972. In a stable courtyard, the Queen examines one of her mounts before saddling up.*

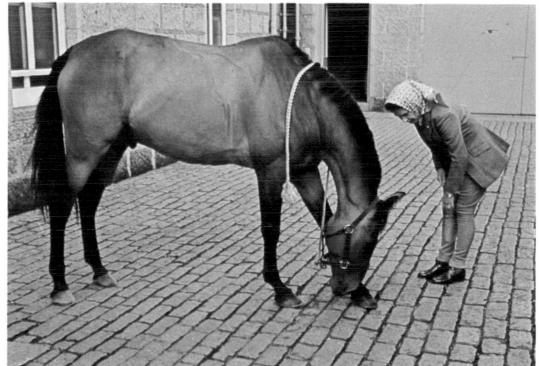

left *This charming, informal photograph of the royal couple by Patrick Lichfield was taken at Balmoral in October 1972 to commemorate the Queen's Silver Wedding.*

right *The Garter Service is held annually at St George's Chapel, Windsor. Seen here in June 1965, the Queen, as Sovereign of the Order, attended by her pages of honour, is about to enter the car after the service.*

After Christmas at Windsor, Prince Philip took his elder children, Prince Charles and Princess Anne, on a skiing holiday to Liechtenstein. This pocket sovereign state, between Switzerland and Austria, amounting only to sixty-five square miles is ruled by Prince Franz Josef II, and has the largest royal family in Europe – over fifty princes and princesses. On the following day, the Queen and Queen Mother took the two young Princes, Andrew and Edward, for their winter holiday at Sandringham.

On 1st February 1966 the Queen and Prince Philip left London Airport for their Caribbean tour, and arrived in a warmer clime at Bridgetown, capital of Barbados, later that day. There have been extensive constitutional changes in the West Indies and Guiana, but all the states wished to continue their membership of the Commonwealth. (Barbados was to achieve independence in November of 1966.) From here the couple went to Georgetown, capital of British Guiana, the only Commonwealth country situated within the South American continent, where the Queen addressed the Legislative Assembly. In May that year this country, one of our largest and most turbulent colonies, reverted to its ancient name of Guyana on becoming an independent member of the Commonwealth. Elizabeth and Philip sailed in the royal yacht *Britannia* to Trinidad, and then to the sister island of Tobago, twenty

miles to the north east, where they landed at Scarborough. They visited several other islands including the Bahamas, not strictly part of the Caribbean, where they attended a service in Nassau Cathedral, before reaching Jamaica, where the Queen opened parliament at Kingston. Elizabeth flew back to London on 11th March, while Philip left for Bermuda en route for the United States.

The first annual list of those selected to receive the new Queen's Award to Industry was announced on the Queen's birthday, 21st April 1966. The Prime Minister had previously accepted the recommendations of the Duke of Edinburgh's Committee to devise a scheme to reward those firms whose performance in either export or technological achievement had been outstanding. The emblem for this scheme was designed by Abram Games, based on Charles I's crown representing both English and Scottish monarchy.

From 9th to 13th May the Queen and Prince Philip made their state visit to King Baudouin and Queen Fabiola of the Belgians, and opened the Churchill Dock at Antwerp. While in Belgium they paid a private visit to the King's father, former King Leopold and his wife Liliane, before going on to Liège. They visited Ypres and Flanders battlefields, scenes of so much slaughter in the First World War before returning home to be hosts to the President of Austria and Frau Jonas.

On 10th July the royal couple attended the World Cup Final at Wembley, when the Queen presented the Jules Rimet Trophy to Bobby Moore, captain of the victorious English team who beat Western Germany four goals to two. The Queen went to Balmoral at the beginning of August, while Philip took Anne to the Commonwealth Games at Kingston, Jamaica. On 6th September both the Queen and Philip entertained the visiting Commonwealth delegates to dinner at St James's Palace, with other members of the royal family present. Two days later they opened the new bridge over the Severn estuary, which created a direct route between Southern England and South Wales, before going on to the British Aircraft Corporation works at Filton, to see the second prototype of the supersonic aircraft Concord (now in service and spelt Concorde).

Alexei Kosygin, the Soviet leader who had replaced Khrushchev, arrived on an official visit in February 1967. During the week he was in Britain, he expressed a wish to disband the NATO and Warsaw alliances, but more constructive was his agreement to establish a teletype line between the Kremlin and 10 Downing Street. In deference to his prejudice against formal dress, the Queen broke a long-standing tradition and allowed lounge suits and short dresses to be worn at the banquet held in his honour at Buckingham Palace, although at a similar banquet in Paris General De Gaulle had insisted on formal dress and white ties. Kosygin said he would be delighted if 'Her Majesty the Queen of Great Britain were to come to the Soviet Union', but this visit has not yet taken place.

At the end of the month, Francis Chichester arrived at Plymouth in his yacht *Gypsy Moth IV*, concluding his epic solo voyage round the world, returning through the dangerous waters round Cape Horn. It had been intended that he should sail from Plymouth to Greenwich, where the Queen was to knight him, but owing to his illness the investiture was delayed until 7th July. Not far from Deptford, where Elizabeth I knighted Sir Francis Drake, Elizabeth II, with the same sword, dubbed Sir Francis Chichester, who received the appointment of a Knight Commander of the British Empire.

above *At Sotheby's in June 1966, the Queen thoughtfully surveys 'Upright Interior Form' by Henry Moore.*

far left *The Battle of Britain Thanksgiving Service in Westminster Abbey in September 1965 was attended by the Queen who unveiled a memorial to Sir Winston Churchill.*

below *Commonwealth Prime Ministers entertained at St James's Palace in September 1966.*

left *Then an impressive model, now a supersonic airliner in service, Concorde is explained to the Queen during her visit to the Filton Works, Bristol, in September 1966.*

right *With the sword used by Queen Elizabeth I to knight Sir Francis Drake in 1581, Queen Elizabeth II dubs Sir Francis Chichester at the Royal Naval College, Greenwich, after his epic single-handed voyage around the world in Gypsy Moth IV.*

below *A plaque to commemorate the 100th anniversary of the birth of Queen Mary is unveiled by her grand-daughter on the wall of Marlborough House in June 1967. The ceremony was attended by Queen Mary's eldest son, the Duke of Windsor, whose wife was making her first public royal appearance.*

On 7th June the Queen unveiled a plaque in a wall of Marlborough House Gardens, London, to commemorate the 100th anniversary of the birth of her grandmother, Queen Mary, the much loved consort of King George V. Mary had lived at Marlborough House as Queen Dowager till her death in 1953. The Duke and Duchess of Windsor flew from Paris for the ceremony, which was attended by 100 guests.

That month, the Queen and Prince Philip flew out to Ottawa, arriving late in the afternoon of 29th June to attend the centenary celebrations of the Canadian Confederation, held on 1st July. At the ceremony, held in open air on Parliament Hill, in a speech broadcast to the Canadian people, the Queen paid tribute to the imagination and sense of duty of men who 100 years ago 'Sitting round a table', had planned the beginnings of the Canadian nation. In the afternoon she attended a party given for thousands of children, cutting the cake in celebration, and then going on to a programme of athletics, dancing and singing in the New Stadium at Lansdowne Park, Ottawa.

On the next day the Queen and Prince Philip attended a service at Christ Church Cathedral, and then boarded the royal yacht *Britannia* at Cornwall to sail down the St Lawrence River to attend the Expo 67 Exhibition, the largest world fair since Britain had originated the idea with the 1851 Exhibition in Crystal Palace. The Exhibition was held on St Helen's and Notre Dame Islands in the St Lawrence River opposite Montreal, and the nations represented vied with each other in the magnificence of their pavilions. The British pavilion was designed by Sir Basil Spence and erected at a cost of two-and-a-half million pounds; the United States pavilion had a dome more than 200 feet high; and Canada's own pavilion, known as the Katimavik (Eskimo for meeting place), was an inverted pyramid over 100 feet high.

The royal party landed at St Lambert Lock on the 3rd July in pouring rain, the only bad weather during this visit, and drove to the Exhibition, where they toured the pavilions of Britain, Quebec, Ontario, the Indians of Canada, Western Provinces and Atlantic Provinces. They had lunch in the Canadian Pavilion, where the Queen congratulated the Canadian people on their remarkable achievement. After lunch the royal party toured the pavilion, and in the evening entertained leading members of the Federal and Quebec Governments, civic dignitaries of Montreal, and the senior officials of Expo 67 and their wives.

On 5th July, the couple sailed to Kingston, Ontario, where, on board the yacht, Philip presented gold awards to fifty recipients of the Duke of Edinburgh Awards Scheme. They then drove back to Ottawa to the ceremony of swearing in the provincial premiers as Privy Counsellors. In the afternoon they attended a military parade to present colours to certain regiments, and visited the site of the National Arts Fund then under construction, where there was a programme of music and drama connected with the project.

After a dinner party that evening at Government House, to which 100 distinguished Canadians were invited, they drove, still in evening dress, to board their aircraft to fly back to Britain.

A fortnight after the state opening of Parliament at Westminster on 31st October, the Queen and Philip went to Malta to make their contribution towards healing the quarrel which had developed earlier in the year over the accelerated run-down of British defence expenditure in Malta, a policy which put many jobs on the island at risk. This was the first time the Queen had visited Malta since its independence in 1964, and she welcomed the opportunity to revisit the scenes of her earlier life as a naval officer's wife, when her father was King. Everywhere the royal couple went they were welcomed. They spent a day with the Navy, crossing the sea to the Island of Gozo, and as the Queen said goodbye to the Governor-General and his wife, she said, 'It's been wonderful'. They returned to Luton Airport on the 17th to spend a weekend with their friends the Wernhers at Luton Hoo.

On 1st December the Queen travelled to the Royal Greenwich Observatory at Herstmonceux, Sussex, to inaugurate the great 98-inch telescope named Isaac Newton, which had cost one million pounds to build. She said, 'It is often said that our most brilliant young men are tempted to leave the country and join the brain-drain because of the lack of first-class equipment for them to work here. The Isaac Newton telescope is a move to counter this in so far as astronomy is concerned'. She went on to say, 'Possibly the main reason for the appeal of astronomy is that man has always been drawn to look upward at the stars, believing he may find somewhere amongst them some clue to his own existence'. Sir Richard Woolley, then the Astronomer Royal, presented the Queen with a working model of the telescope.

On 20th December, two days before the Queen and the rest of the royal family went to spend Christmas at Windsor, Prince Charles flew off with Harold Wilson to Australia to represent her at the memorial service for their Prime Minister Harold Holt, who had drowned. This was the first official visit undertaken by the Prince of Wales.

The Royal Air Force had been formed in 1918, by the union

of the Royal Flying Corps with the Royal Naval Air Service, and the Golden Jubilee of its inception was celebrated on 18th April 1968. The day was marked by a special banquet and reception at Lancaster House, at which the Queen, Prince Philip, the Queen Mother, Princess Margaret, the Duchess of Gloucester and Princess Marina, Duchess of Kent attended, with 200 Royal Air Force and Women's Royal Air Force officers, airmen and airwomen. As the party entered Lancaster House they saw on display a floodlit Gloster Gladiator aircraft similar to *Faith*, *Hope* and *Charity*, the three famous biplanes of the Malta siege, while inside was the Schneider Trophy, lent by the Royal Aero Club.

On 14th June the Queen and Prince Philip travelled by road to Royal Air Force, Abingdon, where they were joined by the Queen Mother, the Duchess of Gloucester and Princess Marina, Duchess of Kent, to attend a massive Royal Air Force review, consisting of a display in the air and on the ground representing past and present achievements of the service. After the Queen had taken the royal salute, the party toured an exhibition hangar and then watched a parade of aircraft, with a demonstration by free-fall parachutists and a fly-past of modern and vintage aircraft.

On the morning of 10th July, at a private ceremony at Buckingham Palace, the Queen knighted Alec Rose after he had sailed his ketch *Lively Lady* solo round the world. He had arrived at Portsmouth, his home town, on 4th July. After the investiture he lunched with the Queen and Prince Philip. Like Sir Francis Chichester's earlier voyage, his epic feat of 318 days captured the attention of the world.

Princess Marina, Duchess of Kent, the Queen's dearly loved

left Prince Charles and Princess Anne attend the Opening of Parliament for the first time in October 1967. Here they stand on either side of the Queen and Prince Philip, as she rises from the throne in the House of Lords after making her speech.

above right Another royal first—this time the first occasion a reigning sovereign has travelled on the London Underground. Here the Queen is shown the driver's cab after opening a new section of the Victoria line in March 1969.

right President Nixon is greeted by Prince Charles at Buckingham Palace in this scene later enjoyed by millions as part of the 1969 royal film.

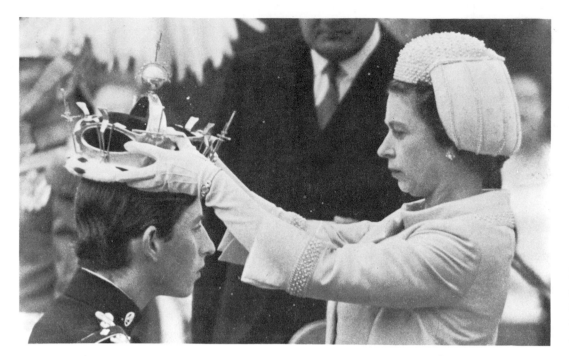

aunt, died on 27th August in her sleep at her home in Kensington Palace, from an inoperable tumour of the brain. She was aged sixty-one. It was a shock, as the public had been unaware of her illness. She appeared comparatively well until two days before her death, when she became unconscious. The Queen, Philip and Charles flew from Scotland to attend her funeral in St George's Chapel, Windsor. She was buried close to Frogmore mausoleum, where on the previous day the Queen had arranged for the late Duke's body to be transferred from St George's to lie at her side. Among other members of the royal family present were the Queen Mother and the Duke of Windsor. A memorial service was held for Princess Marina in Westminster Abbey on 25th October, two months after her death. Millions of people viewed the service on television and mourned the passing of a well-loved lady.

On 1st November the Queen left London Airport on her first Latin American tour, making state visits to Brazil and Chile. This was fortunate timing, for Lord Chalfont was having trade talks with these countries, and the Queen made the royal yacht available to businessmen for their trade discussions. She arrived at Recife Airport, where she was met by Prince Philip, who had flown from the Olympic Games in Mexico. The couple then drove the eight miles to Recife, third city of Brazil, in different cars, she with the provincial Governor and he with the Governor's wife. It was unfortunate that while at Recife the lights failed all over the city. The Queen laughingly told her hosts that the same thing had happened at Covent Garden a week ago, when the television film on the royal family was being made.

Later the royal couple sailed in *Britannia* for Salvador de Bahia, Brazil's one-time capital, and then, via Rio de Janeiro, the country's greatest city, flew to the new capital of Brasilia, where they were welcomed by the President, Marshal Artur de Costa e Silva, and his wife. At the banquet the Queen referred to the times when British and Brazilian history had been linked. 'It was a squadron of the British Navy which escorted King John VI from Portugal to Brazil, and more recently Brazil and the Commonwealth stood side by side in two world wars to defend those principles to which we are equally

dedicated'. The couple spent two days at São Paulo, where the Queen inaugurated the museum of modern art, and then after a visit to a ranch, flew back to tour Rio, one of the world's most beautiful cities.

The next morning the couple left by air for Santiago, capital of Chile, arriving on 11th November. The Queen, in replying to the mayor's welcome, reminded him that, 'The name of your city corresponds to St James in English, the name of my Court in London'. She addressed the Chilean National Congress, while Philip visited the world's largest underground copper mine at El Teniente in the Andes mountains.

On returning to Santiago the Queen went to the races, where she presented a cup for the Isabel II (her name in Spanish) Stakes, while Philip played polo. Their host, President Frei, saw them off on the 18th on their departure by air for Recife. They spent the night in the royal yacht before crossing to Dakar in West Africa on their way back to Britain.

The Queen and Prince Philip arrived at Buckingham Palace at midnight on 19th November, just in time to celebrate their twenty-first wedding anniversary. On 17th December they went with Prince Charles to Cardiff to visit the Castle and National Museum, and the Queen opened the Royal Mint, which had moved from London to its new site at Llantrisant. Here she struck the first decimal coins to be produced there. The following day Elizabeth entertained the King and Queen of Tonga for luncheon at Buckingham Palace. The King had succeeded his mother Queen Salote almost three years earlier.

On 25th February 1969 the Queen and Philip entertained to lunch President Nixon of the United States, with Prince Charles and Princess Anne present, and on 7th March the Queen opened the latest section of the Victoria line on the London underground railway. After declaring Green Park Station open, she travelled the new line to Oxford Circus and returned to Victoria to unveil a commemorative plaque.

On 5th May the Queen and Prince Philip flew to Vienna for their state visit to President and Frau Jonas of Austria. Princess Anne, who was to accompany them, went down with 'flu, and missed the first part of the visit. The couple arrived at the airport with the temperature in the eighties, and attended a magnificent state banquet at the Hofburg Palace. Here the Queen said, 'The word welcome is often used without much feeling. The kindness of your words this evening, together with the deeply moving reception given to us by the people of Vienna have reminded me what welcome really means'. The couple went on to a gala reception at the Schönbrunn Palace, completed in 1713 and one-time home of the Empress Maria Theresa. On the following day they saw the crown jewels of the Holy Roman Empire, attended a performance of the Vienna Spanish Riding School, and visited St Stephen's Cathedral and the Houses of Parliament.

Before the Queen and Philip left Vienna they saw a performance of *Die Fledermaus* at the opera and went on a sight-seeing tour of the ancient city. The party went by special train to Innsbruck and Salzburg, then on by air to Graz. They drove to the Piber Federal Stud, where the Queen stayed for an hour-and-a-half, and returned to London on 10th May, having confirmed the good relations existing between Austria and Britain.

The royal family film, a joint BBC and Independent Television venture, of which shooting had begun a year earlier, was first shown by the BBC on 21st June. Produced by Richard Cawston, it had evolved from a suggestion by Lord Mountbatten and his son-in-law Lord Brabourne after the success of the former's television serial of his life and times in India. The Queen's official life and work was depicted, but the most interesting part of the film was devoted to the private family life of the Queen and Prince Philip. There were glimpses of life at Balmoral, including a picnic by the loch with their children. We saw the Queen and Charles preparing a salad, while Philip and Anne grilled sausages and a steak. Then the Queen took Edward to a village shop for ice cream. In another scene President Nixon was pictured saying to Prince Charles, 'I've seen you on television.' 'I've seen you too', answered Charles.

Twenty-three million people watched the first showing, and when repeated a week later, an audience of fifteen million saw the film. The Queen's fear that this programme, followed by the lengthy showing of the Prince of Wales' investiture, would 'over-expose' the royal family on television, resulted in the announcement that there would be no Christmas message broadcast that year.

The foremost ceremony of 1969 was undoubtedly the investiture of Prince Charles as the twenty-first Prince of Wales at Caernarvon Castle, an event which in splendour vied almost with the Coronation. The ceremony, on 1st July, was planned by the Earl Marshal, the late Duke of Norfolk, assisted by Lord Snowdon as Constable of Caernarvon Castle, and many others. This was the first state occasion to be televised in full, making a three-hour programme which it was estimated was seen by five hundred million viewers. The supreme moment came when the Queen invested and crowned Charles as Prince, who, kneeling before her, paid homage, with his hands placed between hers, while mother and son exchanged the kiss of fealty.

Though the religious service and the Presentation of the Prince to the People were Lloyd George's innovations in 1911 for the investiture of the Queen's uncle (later Duke of Windsor) as Prince of Wales, the main ceremonial has hardly altered through the centuries.

From 15th to 19th July the Queen was host to President Urho Kekkonen of Finland, and on the 28th she travelled by train to Torquay, with Philip, Charles and Anne, to embark in *Britannia*. In Torbay she reviewed the Western Fleet (an amalgamation of the Mediterranean and Home Fleets), and visited several of the thirty-nine ships. On the following day, on board HMS *Eagle*, she gave new colours to the Fleet, which later steamed past in salute.

The Queen went to Hull with Philip and Anne on the 4th August to open the Queen Elizabeth Dock and tour the city before embarking in *Britannia* for the Shetlands for a seven-hour visit. Two days later the couple took all four of their children on a private visit to the King of Norway, the first time the whole family had been together on a foreign holiday. The two boys, Andrew and Edward, were given passports for the trip. The party was met at sea by King Olaf, in his royal yacht *Norge*, who boarded *Britannia* for breakfast before landing at Bergen. The two yachts sailed for Andalsnes, past the island of Veøy, the reputed home of the Queen's ancestor Rognvald the Mighty, father of the first Duke of Normandy, and then on to Molde. The party docked at Trondheim on the 10th and disembarked. Nearby they were entertained for lunch by the Prime Minister, at his farm. The Queen and her young sons left Trondheim two days later to sail back to Scotland, while Philip, Charles and Anne sailed in the fjords in *Bloodhound* for a few more days.

The royal family celebrated a quiet Christmas at Windsor in 1969, for on the 5th December, Prince Philip's mother, the eighty-four year old Princess Alice (Princess Andrew of Greece) died at Buckingham Palace, where she had lived for two years. Her funeral was held five days afterwards at St George's Chapel, Windsor.

THE CONTEMPORARY SEVENTIES

Towards the end of February 1970 the Queen unveiled her new portrait by Annigoni at the National Portrait Gallery, London. This depicted her in the rose pink mantle of Sovereign of the Order of the British Empire. Annigoni's previous portrait of Elizabeth in Garter robes, painted sixteen years earlier and commissioned by the Worshipful Company of Fishmongers, was considered her best likeness, and its successor has not been received with as much enthusiasm. Annigoni owes his introduction to the royal family to Philip's cousin, Queen Helen of Roumania.

Less than a week after the unveiling, a tour of Australasia was planned, and on 2nd March the Queen, accompanied by Princess Anne, left for Vancouver Airport, where she was met by Prince Philip, who had been to the American space centre at Cape Kennedy. The party flew on to Fiji, where they embarked in *Britannia*. After calling in at Tonga, they arrived on 12th March at Wellington, New Zealand where Prince Charles joined them.

This was a tour with a difference; its great success was due partly to the presence of the Queen's elder children, and also the widespread viewing of films of the royal family and the investiture of the Prince of Wales. It will be chiefly remembered, however, for the informality which surrounded the visit. This was the Queen's first 'walkabout' tour, and she talked to hundreds of people at random, her walks taking her over twenty miles of pavements, tracks and grasslands. Charles and Anne concentrated on talking to some of the many thousands of children who clustered to see them everywhere along the route.

The Queen opened the New Zealand Parliament on 13th March and later sailed with her family to South Island. After visiting Picton for a walkabout, they watched the re-enactment of Captain Cook's landing at Ship Cove in Queen Charlotte's Sound 200 years earlier. Charles and Anne spent an informal weekend at the Mount Peel Sheep Station before joining their parents at Christchurch.

On North Island, after a three-day visit to Auckland, the royal party flew to Hamilton, where the tour ended with a banquet. They then rested for two days on board *Britannia*

before the yacht returned to Auckland, and the party flew to Sydney to start their tour of Australia at the beginning of April.

They toured the island of Tasmania before going on to Melbourne and Sydney, when Prince Charles took the opportunity of showing Timbertop to his sister, thereafter flying to Japan to visit the Expo 70 Exhibition. The rest of the family flew up to Brisbane, arriving on 12th April. Here the crowds were so thick that Philip had to ask the police to stand back, because, as he said, 'The people can't see'. The party had a pleasant trip to the Great Barrier Reef, and at Cookstown watched a pageant of Cook's landing from the *Endeavour*, in which the Torres Strait Islanders formed the guard of honour.

From Canberra they flew to Sydney at the end of the month to attend further celebrations of Captain Cook's landing, before leaving on 3rd May for a flight home via Canada, arriving at London Airport on the following day.

On 5th July the Queen, Prince Philip and Princess Anne began their tour of the North West Territories of Canada and the Province of Manitoba, both of which were celebrating their centenaries. The Queen particularly wished to visit both, as she had had to curtail her visits during her last Canadian tour due to the impending birth of Prince Andrew.

At Frobisher Bay on Baffin Island the party was joined by Prince Charles to undertake a tour through more than 2,000

miles of the frozen north. The Queen turned the first sod on the site of a new Cathedral to be built in the form of an igloo at Frobisher Bay. At Tuktoyaktuk on the Arctic Ocean, lying to the south of the North Pole, the family watched an Eskimo drum dance, and saw the midnight sun. At Yellowknife, Prince Charles and Princess Anne attended a barbecue, and the royal party received presents of a polar bear rug, a walrus ivory, white fox furs and a painting of an Arctic seascape. When Prince Charles was asked to kiss the winner of a beauty contest, he mischievously enquired, 'May I see her first, and may I choose where I kiss her?'

At Fort Smith, the royal party attended a buffalo barbecue, and afterwards Prince Philip and his son visited mines at Pine Point, while the Queen and her daughter went to an old-timers' reunion. The final two days of the tour were spent at Winnipeg, capital of Manitoba, where the Queen addressed an outside assembly of the Manitoba Legislature, watched by 25,000 people. During her stay in the province the Queen spoke to Indians at The Pas, the French-speaking Canadians at Saint Pierre, where she declared that she had received, 'A most vivid impression of an intricate racial, religious and cultural tapestry which makes up the population of the province'. She presented the trophy at the Manitoba Derby held on the Assiniboia Downs, and before leaving for Britain, expressed to the Lieutenant-Governor her warmest good wishes for the province's next 100 years. The family arrived back at London Airport on 15th July, except for Charles and Anne, who flew to Washington to stay with the Nixons for four days at the White House.

On Christmas Day 1970, the Queen resumed her traditional talk on television and radio, which had been omitted the pre-

vious year. This was the first time that Prince Philip, Prince Charles and Princess Anne all appeared. The broadcast took place in the Queen's sitting room in Buckingham Palace, although shots of New Zealand, Australia, Canada and the Commonwealth Games in Edinburgh the previous July were also included. In this new format the emphasis of the broadcast was on the Commonwealth. The Queen said, 'During the course of these visits we met and talked with a great number of people of every sort of occupation and living in every kind of community and climate, yet in all this diversity they had one thing in common, they were all members of the Commonwealth family . . .'

Less than ten months after their last Canadian tour, on 3rd May 1971 the Queen, Prince Philip and Princess Anne visited British Columbia for the province's centennial celebrations. They arrived at Vancouver Airport, and joined *Britannia* to sail for the capital, Victoria, where the tour officially began. Tens of thousands of spectators crowded the Inner Harbour area to watch the royal yacht dock.

The party visited the gold rush country, where a century before thousands of prospectors had swarmed along Wild Horse Creek to dig and pan for gold. At Fort Steel the Queen showed a special interest in the *Dunrobin*, a steam engine built in Glasgow in 1895 which had carried her father, grandfather and great-grandfather. At Williams Lake, in the heart of the caribou cattle-ranching region, the party watched a minia-ture rodeo. In the dirt ring a bull named *Tomahawk*, weighing a ton, horned in on the press, and with the bull thundering at their heels, the journalists leapt up the fence and through the gate, while cowboys grabbed at the bucking beast. Seated in their stand overlooking the ring, the Queen and Prince Philip

burst into laughter as they craned forward to watch the scramble for safety. On Sunday 9th May Prince Philip read the lesson at the service in St John's United Church, Westview, where there had been some doubt among tour officials about whether the Church plate should be passed to the royal visitors. They eventually decided that it should.

In August the Queen and Prince Philip gave Princess Anne her twenty-first birthday party aboard *Britannia* at Portsmouth. Philip accompanied Charles and Anne to Hamble to meet Chay Blyth on his return from sailing single-handed round the world from east to west in his ketch *British Steel*. Three days later, on 9th August, the royal party sailed north to Scotland, driving from Thurso to have lunch with the Queen Mother at the Castle of Mey. A week later they left *Britannia* at Aberdeen to drive to Balmoral.

On 5th October 1971 Emperor Hirohito and his Empress Nagako arrived at Gatwick Airport for their state visit, the first time an Emperor had left Japan. There had been some criticism when the Queen had restored the Order of the Garter to the Emperor, which had been removed during the war, and his visit aroused controversy, especially among servicemen or ex-servicemen who had fought against Japan during the Second World War. Following the state banquet at Buckingham Palace, the Emperor entertained his guests at the Japanese Embassy, and during their visit he and his wife visited the London Zoological Gardens, the Natural History Museum and the British Museum.

Ten days after the Emperor and Empress had left London, the Queen, Prince Philip and Princess Anne flew on a state visit to Turkey. At Ankara, the capital, they saw the tomb of Kemal Ataturk, architect of modern Turkey. After the state banquet given by President and Madame Sunay, and the dinner in their honour at the British Embassy, the royal party flew to Izmir for a night on board the royal yacht. They travelled fifty miles to the south to see the ruins of Ephesus, one of the twelve Ionic cities of Asia Minor, saw the Gallipoli battlefields where so many Anzac soldiers had fallen in the First World War, and toured the sights of Istanbul, the former Turkish capital. The Queen flew back to London Airport on 25th October, while Prince Philip travelled to Germany to visit Army units there, and Princess Anne flew to Hong Kong.

After the bombing outrage at the Post Office Tower in London, warnings had been received that the next target would be the Victoria Tower, at the Houses of Parliament, through which the Queen would pass during her State Opening of Parliament on 2nd November. The most massive security arrangements ever to be mounted were carried out, during which the vaults under the Houses of Parliament were searched as thoroughly as they had been 350 years earlier when Guy Fawkes' barrels of gunpowder were discovered. Fortunately, the opening proceeded without incident, and it was remarked that the Queen had looked as self-assured as ever.

Early in 1972, on 24th January, Prince Philip represented the Queen at the funeral of King Frederick of Denmark at Roskilde Cathedral, which was soon followed by the royal couple's strenuous South-East Asian tour. A week before they left her doctors advised the Queen to have a complete rest, and she cancelled her engagements. The royal party, which included Princess Anne, flew on the 8th February to tour the ancient oriental kingdom of Thailand, previously known as Siam. They boarded *Britannia* in the Gulf of Thailand and, after

right *In a splendid golden chariot drawn by forty men, the Queen, Prince Philip and Princess Anne with the Sultan and Sultana of Brunei, are carried through the streets of Bandar Seri Begawan, the capital of Brunei, on the royal visit to the island of Borneo in March 1972.*

far right *In contrast to the splendour of the Far East, the Queen strolls through the ancient streets of Arles after watching a display of traditional Provençal dancing, on her state visit to France in May 1972.*

an overnight cruise, met their hosts King Bhumibol and Queen Sirikit, who showed them the magnificent sights of the capital, Bangkok. After flying to visit the northern city of Chiang Mai, they rejoined the royal yacht at Bangkok for a three-day voyage to Singapore, where they met the British-educated Prime Minister, Lee Kuan Yew. After inspecting troops, the royal party sailed for Malaysia, arriving on 20th February in the capital of Kuala Lumpur. During their tour of Malaysia they visited the island of Borneo, touring Sabah, Brunei and Sarawak. At Kuching, in Sarawak, there was a spectacular landing in long boats, but unfortunately half the royal escort boats capsized in a storm.

When the royal party returned to Singapore, Anne travelled back to London, and the Queen and Prince Philip undertook a six-hour sightseeing tour of Malacca and other Malaysian towns, including the port of Penang, before sailing for the Maldive Islands in the Indian Ocean.

After four days at sea the Queen and Prince Philip reached the Maldives, an independent state since 1965, and visited the Royal Air Force staging post on the island of Gan. They sailed on to reach the Seychelles on 20th March, where the Queen opened the first airport Four days later the party visited the island of Mauritius, then in a state of emergency due to activities of the left wing. Despite regulations that not more than five people should assemble together, a blind eye was cast on the quarter of a million people in carnival mood who gathered in the streets to see the royal visitors. The tour finished with a four-hour visit to President Jomo Kenyatta of Kenya, who showed the Queen his rose garden after lunch. The Queen flew back to London on 26th March, one of the first engagements on her return being the opening of the Treasures of Tutankhamun Exhibition at the British Museum,

The Queen and Prince Philip flew to Paris on 15th May for their second state visit to France, this time at the invitation of the late President Monsieur Georges Pompidou who had suc-

ceeded General de Gaulle as President in June 1969. British relations with France had been strained for some years, due to de Gaulle's determined opposition to Britain's entry into the Common Market. At the President's state banquet at the Grand Trianon, Versailles, the Queen remarked, 'We may drive on different sides of the road, but we are going the same way'. The banquet was followed by a reception in the state apartments of the Palace of Versailles. Two days later the Queen and Philip flew to tour the South of France, and at Avignon the Queen was joined by Prince Charles, Philip having departed to see a wild game reserve in the Camargue.

When the royal family returned to Paris they took the opportunity to visit the Duke and Duchess of Windsor. The Duke had hoped to greet the couple downstairs but was not well enough to do so, and the Queen went up to his bedroom to see him. That evening the royal party held a banquet at the British Embassy, and the next day, 19th May, they went to see the ancient Norman capital of Rouen, where they visited a war cemetery, before boarding *Britannia* on the Seine to return to Britain. After this successful visit, the British Ambassador, Sir Christopher Soames, summed up current Anglo-French relations by saying, 'We are friends again now, and nothing can go wrong'.

Nine days after the Queen left France, on 28th May the Duke of Windsor died at his home in Paris. The Royal Air Force flew his body back to England and it was taken to St George's Chapel, Windsor to lie in state. Fifty-seven thousand people paid tribute to the former King Edward VIII by quietly filing past his coffin. The Duchess of Windsor arrived on 3rd June to stay at Buckingham Palace. This was the Queen's Official Birthday, and by her command the Trooping the Colour was preceded by a memorial tribute to her uncle consisting of a roll of drums, a minute's silence and a pipers' lament. The ceremonial funeral at St George's Chapel was held two days later. In the Choir the Queen sat next to the

left *Gentle smiles are exchanged during the meeting of the Queen and the Duchess of Windsor in Paris in May 1972. The Queen had just visited her uncle, the Duke of Windsor, who died ten days later.*

right *With the Duke of Beaufort, Master of the Beaufort Hunt, the Queen and Prince Philip, with their children Andrew and Edward and their nephew and niece Lord Linley and Lady Sarah Armstrong-Jones, review the hounds.*

below *Balmoral Castle, the Queen's Scottish home, was rebuilt by the Prince Consort in 1853–5 and commands a magnificent prospect with its massive towers and turrets.*

A Patrick Lichfield photograph taken at Windsor Castle on the occasion of the Queen's silver wedding in November 1972. Present are:

1 The Queen. 2 Lord Snowdon. 3 Duke of Kent. 4 Prince Michael. 5 Prince Philip. 6 Prince Charles. 7 Prince Andrew. 8 Hon Angus Ogilvy. 9 Duchess of Kent. 10 Lord Nicholas Windsor (younger son of Duke of Kent). 11 Earl of St Andrews (elder son of Duke of Kent). 12 Princess Anne. 13 Marina Ogilvy. 14 Princess Alexandra. 15 James Ogilvy. 16 Princess Margaret. 17 The Queen Mother. 18 Lady Sarah Armstrong-Jones. 19 Viscount Linley. 20 Prince Edward. 21 Lady Helen Windsor (daughter of Duke of Kent).

left *The Queen takes the salute at the birthday parade, the climax of the annual Trooping the Colour ceremony, which takes place on Horse Guards Parade in celebration of the Queen's official birthday.*

right *Broad smiles from the Queen and her family as they leave Buckingham Palace on 20th November 1972 for the Thanksgiving Service at Westminster Abbey to celebrate her silver wedding anniversary.*

below *A scene from the service during the singing of a hymn.*

above *Formal salute on the steps to the main entrance of the Parliament Buildings, Wellington, New Zealand, prior to the Queen opening Parliament on 4th February 1974.*

above right *The Queen meets Nureyev, the world renowned ballet dancer and choreographer, at the Royal Variety Performance held at the London Palladium in November 1973. In line and waiting their turn are Ronnie Corbet, Lenny Peters and Cliff Richard.*

bereaved Duchess, to be joined by Prince Philip, who had walked in the procession immediately behind the coffin. The Duke was privately interred at Frogmore, in Windsor Home Park beside the graves of other members of the royal family.

A week later the Grand Duke and Duchess of Luxembourg came to London, and on 8th July the Queen and other members of the royal family attended the wedding of her cousin, Prince Richard of Gloucester, to the Danish Miss Birgitte van

The Queen and Prince Philip returned from Balmoral to Buckingham Palace in mid-October to leave with Princess Anne on their first state visit to a Communist country, Yugoslavia. They received a warm welcome from Marshal Tito and the Yugoslav people, and the tour included an informal walk through Zagreb and a visit to the Marshal's villa in the Brioni Islands, before the party returned to London on the following day.

On 20th November 1972 the Queen and Prince Philip celebrated the twenty-fifth anniversary of their marriage by attending a Thanksgiving Service in Westminster Abbey. Afterwards, with the Queen Mother, Prince Charles and Princess Anne, they were entertained in the Guildhall by the Lord Mayor and Corporation of London. Messages of congratulation flooded into Buckingham Palace from all parts of the world on this happy occasion.

The Queen and Prince Philip left on 25th June 1973 on a twelve-day visit to Canada, to be greeted on their arrival at Toronto by the Prime Minister, Pierre Trudeau. After attending centenary celebrations in Prince Edward Island, they went to Saskatchewan to see the celebrations at Regina for the Royal Canadian Mounted Police. They opened the Calgary Stampede on the 5th July and flew back to London on the following day.

In August that year the Queen and Prince Philip went to Bath and Bristol, and attended the 1,000th anniversary of the crowning at Bath Abbey of their ancestor King Edgar. A slate slab has been inserted in the abbey floor to commemorate their visit. An account of this coronation on Whit Sunday 973, written by an eye-witness, is the earliest we possess. Many elements of the ceremony, including the anthem 'Zadok the Priest' sung during the annointing, were used in the Queen's coronation in 1953, but in English rather than Latin.

The Queen made her six-day visit to Australia on 15th October for two principal reasons, as she said at the Federal Parliament luncheon given in her and Prince Philip's honour at Canberra. The first was to approve her new title, Queen of Australia, to which she gave assent in person to the Act passed by the Australian Parliament on the following day. Referring to the second reason, she then said, amid laughter, 'There was the opening of an opera house somewhere in New South Wales'.

This was the sail-roofed Sydney Opera House, overlooking the Harbour, which had cost one hundred million Australian dollars to build, and had been designed by the Danish

Deurs, whom he had first met when a Cambridge undergraduate. The wedding took place at Barnwell Parish Church, Northamptonshire. The Prince's elder brother, Prince William of Gloucester, was tragically killed, with his co-pilot, in an air crash while taking off as a competitor in the Goodyear Air Race near Northampton. His death resulted in the Queen's announcement that she would not attend the Munich Olympics, to which Prince Philip had gone a day before the accident.

An unusual welcome for the Queen from the formidable and heavily armed Mudmen, one of the fiercest tribes of Papua, New Guinea. During this royal tour in February 1974, the party drove into a stadium at Goroko to see a mass gathering of tribes of the central highlands.

architect Joern Utzen. The Queen and Prince Philip arrived at the Opera House in the afternoon of 20th October for the opening ceremony and a tour of the building, and returned that evening to attend the inaugural concert given by the Sydney Symphony Orchestra, the Philharmonia Choir and the Philharmonia Motet.

A large crowd outside the Opera House on the following day saw the royal couple making a second, unannounced visit. After a film for children finished in the music room, the Queen opened the door. At first the young audience gasped in disbelief, and then started to applaud. The Queen then went backstage to see the sets of 'The Magic Flute', of which the royal party saw a gala performance on the following day.

As part of the Sir Winston Churchill centenary celebrations, on 1st November, the Queen attended the unveiling of a new bronze statue of him in Parliament Square, opposite the Houses of Parliament, in company with Sir Winston's widow, Baroness Spencer-Churchill, and their grandson, Winston Churchill, MP.

On 14th November, the wedding of Princess Anne and Captain Mark Philips took place in Westminster Abbey with all the ceremonial due to a daughter of the Sovereign. The Queen lent the couple the royal yacht *Britannia* for their honeymoon in the Caribbean and the Galapagos Islands, before the ship sailed across the Pacific for the Queen's forthcoming tour.

Just before Christmas Day 1973, the royal family were

alarmed to find that Prince Edward was suffering from appendicitis, and he was driven from Windsor to the Great Ormond Street Children's Hospital in London, but as the doctors decided an operation was unnecessary he was able to return to the Castle. The Queen's 1973 message on Christmas Day included two film sequences. One was a behind-the-scenes view inside Buckingham Palace before the royal family appeared on the balcony after Princess Anne's wedding, and was made by Richard Cawston, whose earlier film on the royal family had been so popular. One scene showed various members of the royal group encouraging Anne and Mark to step on to the balcony by urging, 'Go on, go on!' and the Queen turning to the couple and saying, 'Well if you'd like to . . .' 'All right then', decided Princess Anne, and turning to Prince Edward, who was standing on her bridal gown, she said, 'but get off my dress first'. The other sequence shown was of the recent royal reception at Ottawa for Commonwealth Prime Ministers.

The Queen left Heathrow on 27th January 1974 for her Australian and New Zealand tour, and was joined at Ottawa Airport by Princess Anne and Captain Mark Phillips, who had spent the weekend in Canada. The Queen opened the new International Airport at Raratonga in the Cook Islands, reminding the islanders to treat with caution the changes to their way of life that the new airport would bring.

When the royal party arrived at Christchurch, New Zealand on 30th January they were met by Prince Philip, who had

above left *Pretty curtseys for the Queen from young children of the Royal Academy of Dancing as she leaves after opening the Academy's new headquarters in November 1974.*

above *Surrounded by children again the Queen is welcomed during her successful state visit to Mexico in February 1975.*

right *At Birmingham in March 1975 the Queen visits the emergency services responsible for dealing with the bomb outrages suffered by the city in the previous year. Here she has a remotely controlled 'wheel barrow' anti-bomb device explained to her.*

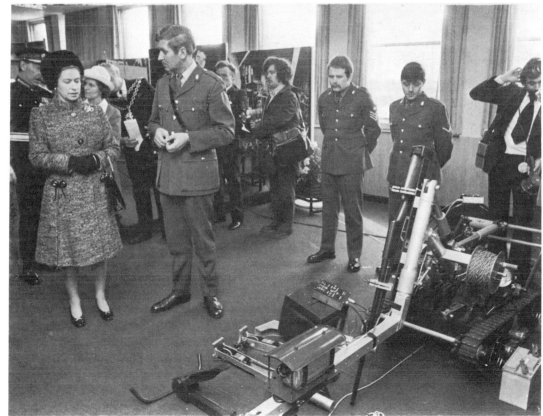

come to open the sixth Commonwealth Games on the previous weekend, and by Prince Charles from the Royal Naval frigate *Jupiter*. 'This is certainly a family gathering,' the Queen said in reply to a welcome by New Zealand's Prime Minister, the late Norman Kirk. 'We are glad to be here, and glad to be together. I am sure the same applies to the great family of the Commonwealth', she added. That evening the family gave a reception and dinner to Games' officials aboard *Britannia*, which had recently undergone a major refit. The yacht was anchored off Lyttelton, fourteen miles from Christchurch, and lay alongside Prince Charles' frigate. The next day the Queen watched the final session of the Games, amidst some boisterous scenes. Some of the competitors, instead of marching round the arena, jumped into the two open Land Rovers in which the royal party were touring the stadium. Any possible criticism was silenced when the Queen later remarked, 'No one who saw the athletes and officials circling the track at the end of the Games, when all barriers were forgotten in general friendship, could doubt the real value of such a gathering'.

The Queen opened the New Zealand Parliament at Wellington on 4th February, for the first time in her new title of Queen of New Zealand, when Captain Phillips fulfilled his new role as the Queen's personal aide-de-camp. She asked for the minimum of formality on her tour, but when the royal party walked round a seaside park and carnival at Nelson, local policemen were powerless to stop the vast crowd from elbowing and jostling each other within two yards of the Queen. It was subsequently announced that royal routes would in future be roped off to give the Queen breathing space and the people a better view.

The royal party visited the famous Rotorua hot springs, and at Waitangi on the evening of 6th February, New Zealand's National Day, they watched a pageant of the nation's history. Two days later they went to Ngaruawahia for the Queen to open a Maori cultural centre in the grounds of the wooden palace of the Queen of the Maoris. That day the royal party embarked at Auckland on the royal yacht to sail for Norfolk Island, which was settled by the descendants of some of the *Bounty* mutineers. As the seas were so rough, it was doubted that the Queen would undertake the half-a-mile passage ashore, but she was determined not to disappoint the islanders on the first visit of a reigning sovereign.

From here, in the second half of February, the royal party toured the New Hebrides, the only condominium (a colony ruled jointly by two powers, in this case by Britain and France) in the world, and then voyaged to the Solomon Islands and Papua New Guinea. This last territory soon afterwards achieved independence within the Commonwealth.

On 27th February the royal family arrived by air in Canberra for the Queen's fifth Australian visit. The next day, after opening Parliament for the first time as Queen of Australia, she had to fly back to London in company with her daughter Princess Anne and Captain Mark Phillips, as events in Britain had led to a general election. Prince Philip was left to con-

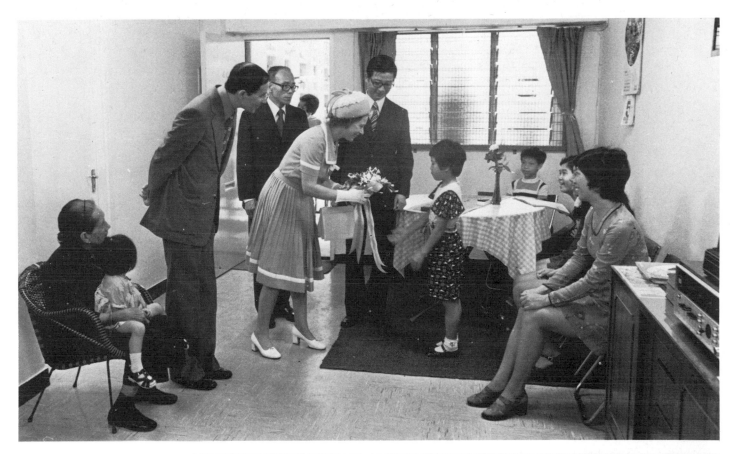

left *In Barbados in February 1975 the royal couple are escorted under tropical palm trees. It was on this visit that the Queen dubbed the cricketer Gary Sobers a knight before an audience of 10,000 excited Barbadians.*

above *The Queen visits the home of ferry-boat ticket collector Mr Tang Shiu-cheung and his family on the Oi Man Estate, Hong Kong, in May 1975. She signed a banner for Mr Shiu-cheung who said he would keep it for the rest of his life.*

right *On the same visit the Queen points out an interesting fruit on her visit to a street market. This was the first visit by a reigning sovereign to the colony since it became associated with the British Crown 134 years ago.*

tinue the scheduled tour on his own until the Queen was able to rejoin him. The general election proved a virtual stalemate, as neither the Conservative nor the Labour Parties achieved an overall majority. Edward Heath attempted to form a Government, but after failing to form a coalition with the Liberal Party, on 4th March he tendered his resignation to the Queen. Less than two hours later the Queen sent for Harold Wilson, who accepted the office later that evening. The protracted timetable of the events required the Queen to cancel the rest of her Australian tour.

After driving by car to open the new session of Parliament, an occasion of austerity contrasting with the usual state openings, the Queen left London Airport on the following day to meet Prince Philip in the island of Bali. It later transpired that her plane came close to being 'downed' as a dummy target by four United States fighter jets over Germany in a NATO exercise, and a full-scale enquiry was ordered.

Prince Philip had visited the exotic island of Bali once before, and he now wished the Queen to share the experience. The couple enjoyed a brief holiday before the Queen's state visit to Indonesia, of which the island forms a part. The royal yacht *Britannia*, with Prince Philip and his uncle Lord Mountbatten on board, arrived from Darwin on the 14th, a few hours before the Queen's plane flew in. The party watched dancing displays, enjoyed the scenery, and while resting in the mountains were surprised to find themselves looking down on a pool formed by a natural spring in which several smiling women were bathing in the nude, while men, similarly unattired, swam in an adjoining pool.

The state visit to Indonesia, the world's third richest nation in natural resources, started on 18th March on the royal party's arrival at Jakarta, the capital. The President, General Suharto,

concerned about riots the previous January at the time of the visit to Japan's Prime Minister, undertook full-scale security arrangements. There were troops everywhere in combat dress and carrying automatic rifles, while jeeps and armoured cars patrolled the streets, and helicopters hovered above.

The Queen's last surviving uncle, the Duke of Gloucester, died at his home at Barnwell, Northamptonshire, on 10th June 1974 after an illness of over three years. His impressive funeral in St George's Chapel four days later was the first to be televised 'live' and in the slow march up the hill, with drums beating, his coffin was escorted by a detachment of combined services, reflecting his full-time Army career. In front of the coffin walked his personal charger, the thirteen-year-old *Bugle Boy* from the Scots Guards' stables. The Queen and the widowed Duchess were the chief mourners in a congregation of 700.

Despite drenching rain, the Queen's twenty-mile cruise on the River Thames aboard the pleasure boat *Windsor Regent* on 18th October proved a great success, enabling many children to see her from the banks and at her various landing points, where she chatted to them for some time. She went on board at Hurley, having first planted a commemorative tree and at Cookham, on returning to the boat, she slipped on a wet gangplank, but was saved from getting wet by an alert waterman. She received the High Steward at Maidenhead, and at Eton Brocas she met the Provost of Eton College. When she landed at Magna Carta Island she was probably the first sovereign to set foot there since King John. She planted a walnut tree to mark the end of the tour, and returned via Wraysbury and Horton to Windsor.

As Sandringham was to undergo repairs, and seventy-three staff rooms no longer required were to be demolished, the

left Continuing her May 1975 tour of the Far East to Japan, the Queen here meets the noted actor Koshiro Matsumoto (second from right). This visit was again the first by a British sovereign and was very popular, some Japanese newspapers proclaiming it 'The most spectacular event since the Emperor's coronation'.

right A week later the Queen was in Greenwich at the Royal Observatory. At the Astronomy Exhibition in the Queen's House, she looks through a 28-inch telescope, seventh largest of this type in the world.

Queen and her family left Windsor after Christmas for a month's holiday at Wood Farm, Wolferton, two miles from the royal residence. The farmhouse, lying near the shore of The Wash, has only eight bedrooms, so space was limited. The Queen Mother and Princess Margaret stayed with their friend Ruth, Lady Fermoy. The holiday ended on Monday 3rd February 1975, but the Queen returned the following Friday for a surprise weekend. An official said, 'She has been very happy at Wood Farm'. That month it was announced that the Queen had abandoned her plans for a full-scale modernization at Sandringham, in view of the country's economic situation, and that the house will eventually be opened to the public. The grounds are already accessible to visitors, of course.

In February the Queen met the men and women of the emergency services who had been involved in the recent wave of bomb explosions in London. She spent fifty minutes at New Scotland Yard, meeting members of the bomb squad who described to her how they deal with terrorist attacks and carry out their investigations to trace the instigators. In the exhibition room she saw a plastic bag filled with gelignite equipped with an alarm-clock detonating device, similar to the first bomb planted in London in 1973. She saw the valuable three-and-half-year-old Labrador called *Mark*, who is expert in sniffing out explosives, and met his handler, Police Constable Malcolm Moore, the pair having searched Westminster Abbey before Princess Anne's wedding.

From the Yard, the Queen visited the London Fire Brigade, where she learnt about methods of dealing with the bombs, and had an informal chat with the foremen. At the Ambulance Headquarters in Waterloo Road, she met the control room staff and spoke to a driver who had been injured by a bomb blast at Chelsea. She next visited the South-Western District

of the Post Office in Victoria, where she met a postman who had lost two fingers while attempting to deliver a parcel which had been boobytrapped.

On 16th February 1975 the Queen and Prince Philip flew to the Caribbean and Mexico. First they visited Bermuda, then in the throes of a general strike, for the Queen's first visit in twenty years, amid security precautions arising from the assassination the previous year of the Governor, Sir Richard Sharples. The general strike caused the itinerary to be amended, and at the entrance of the dockyard the Queen had to cross the nine-man picket line singing to a calypso tune, 'We shall not be moved'. The line stepped aside for the Queen in good humour, one man shouting, 'It's not you, Your Majesty, it's the Government'. Two days later, in Barbados, the Queen dubbed the cricketer Gary Sobers a knight, whereupon the islanders called him 'The Sir of all Sirs'.

During the journey to Mexico the sea proved choppy, and *Britannia* anchored at a yachting harbour some miles from the scheduled point of arrival. At the airport in Mexico City a vast crowd greeted 'la Reina Isabel' on what proved to be the most spectacular royal visit ever.

The Queen received deafening cheers when she helped President Echeverria in the annual Raising of the Flag Ceremony in the central square, the Zocalo, by the Cathedral. It was filled with students waving whisks of red, white and green, the Mexican national colours. One side was filled with a bank of people holding green cards, and on a signal, all these people turned their cards to form an elaborate design showing portraits of the Queen and the President, with between them a heraldic device symbolizing friendship between the two peoples. The great reception in Mexico City was repeated at Veracruz, the port founded by the Spanish conquistadores,

and all the Mexican newspapers, television and radio covered the royal tour in great detail. The Queen returned to London on 2nd March, while Prince Philip went on to visit other Central American countries.

On St George's Day, 23rd April, the Queen and several members of the royal family, including Prince Philip, Prince Andrew, the Queen Mother and Princess Margaret, attended a service of thanksgiving in St George's Chapel, Windsor marking the opening of the celebrations of the Chapel's quincentenary.

Three days later the Queen and Prince Philip left for Jamaica and on arrival, after being received by the Governor-General, they went on a walkabout to meet the people of Kingston. The Queen received the Commonwealth heads of Government assembled for the Conference, which she opened. She also opened the new law school, named after Norman Manley, the late Prime Minister, which is attached to the University of the West Indies. This was the first law school to be established in the West Indies, and enabled those who wished to train as lawyers to do so without making the journey to Britain.

The royal party left Jamaica on 30th April for Honolulu for a brief private stay before the rigours of their Far Eastern tour. Thousands of people welcomed the Queen's arrival in Hong Kong on 4th May, both at Kai Tak Airport on the mainland and on the main jetty on Hong Kong Island, to see the first reigning sovereign to visit the colony in the 134 years it has been associated with the British Crown – they called her their 'Lui Wong' (Woman King). This was an auspicious day, for her Chinese subjects were celebrating Tin Hau (the Goddess of Heaven), protector of fishermen and sailors. The royal party saw, in the words of the Governor, Sir Murray Maclehose, '... the best of Hong Kong as well as its blemishes'. The Queen and her husband went separate ways to cover as many institutions and areas as possible, while the security forces kept discreetly in the background to allow them to mix as freely as possible with the people.

When the Queen, with Prince Philip, arrived in Japan on the morning of 7th May, she was to make the first state visit of a British sovereign. Tokyo was crowded with visitors despite a train strike, and the royal visitors were welcomed with great enthusiasm, seeing features of both modern and ancient Japan. On attending a luncheon given by the president of Keidanren, the Japanese equivalent of the Confederation of British Industry, the Queen said that the number of businessmen and tourists travelling between the two countries had grown from a trickle to a flood. She added, 'British industry is now giving serious attention to the large and growing Japanese market, and Japanese goods and products are well known and popular in Britain. I hope that trade will flourish for its own sake, but still more because it is, and will be, the mainspring of Anglo-Japanese relations'.

In the Akasaka Palace the Queen removed her shoes to enter a Japanese-style house with grass mats, and watched a display of Ikebana, the Japanese art of flower arrangement. The royal party visited the principal shrine of the Shinto religion at Ise, dedicated to Amaterasu, the sun goddess. The shrine consists of three wooden stockades, one inside the other, in the heart of a pine wood. The Queen and Prince Philip, were taken into the first and second stockades, but only the Emperor, who was not present, is allowed to enter the innermost stockade.

The informality of our royal family, compared to their own, greatly impressed the Japanese. Journalists called the visit 'The most spectacular event since the Emperor's coronation'. Several newspapers described the Queen as 'Britain's most elegant saleswoman'. She and Prince Philip arrived home in London on 13th May.

A picturesque occasion took place a week later, when the Queen and Prince Philip went by water to Greenwich to mark the 300th anniversary of the founding of the Royal Observatory, celebrated appropriately during European Heritage Year. The Observatory had moved to Herstmonceux, Sussex, in 1958, but at the Astronomy Exhibition, held in the Queen's House, the Queen inaugurated the twenty-eight inch telescope, the seventh largest of this type in the world. After lunch in the Painted Hall, the couple toured the town of Greenwich and visited the *Cutty Sark* before returning to Westminster Pier by hydrofoil.

Westminster Abbey was the scene of a magnificent ceremonial on 28th May, when the Queen installed her son as Great Master and eight new Knights Grand Cross of the Most Honourable Order of the Bath, at a service to celebrate the 250th anniversary of the refounding of this Order. The procession of eighty-five Knights Grand Cross and one Dame Grand Cross, in company with their sovereign and the New Grand Master, all in their crimson mantles, passed through the Abbey's aisles and nave into the Henry VII Chapel, which is the Chapel of the Order.

May 1975 proved a sad month for the Queen. The death occurred of Lady Margaret Hay, who had been one of her ladies-in-waiting since 1947, and thus was the longest serving member of her Household. This was followed a week later by that of Lord Plunket, first her equerry and later Deputy Master of the Household. Both had served her loyally throughout her reign.

The Queen, appropriately wearing a flower-printed dress, opened the new Covent Garden Market, south of the River Thames, in June 1975. On her two-hour walk she chatted with traders and porters in the sixty-eight acre site at Nine Elms, Vauxhall, and revealed that Prince Charles has an ugli every morning for breakfast and that she herself likes the kiwi fruit.

far left *Sporting a sprig of oak leaves on Oak Apple Day (5th June 1975), the Queen has a word with ninety-three year old Bill Avery, the oldest Chelsea Pensioner on parade at the Annual Founder's Day Parade at the Royal Chelsea Hospital. Oak Apple Day commemorates the restoration of Charles II who founded the hospital.*

right *During a visit to Fleet Street in February 1976, the Queen switches on a press to start a newspaper run.*

While the Queen visited one end of the vast fruit and vegetable market, Philip toured the other. Hundreds of market workers and their families heard the Queen say, 'I hope the humour and efficiency of the old market, which is legendary, can survive the transfer to the new premises. It was a sad day when the market had to move from its famous old home, but it provides a vital service and must have the best possible facilities'.

The twenty-nine-year-old King Carl Gustav of Sweden, who had succeeded his grandfather in 1973, paid a state visit to the Queen at Edinburgh on 8th July. During his time in Scotland he attended the beating the retreat ceremony with his hosts, who included the Queen Mother, Prince Charles and Princess Margaret.

Also in July, the Queen and Prince Philip visited the Silverwood Colliery in Yorkshire, and went 1,800 feet below ground to see for themselves what a miner's work is really like. Wearing a helmet and white overalls, the Queen descended in the cage to the pit bottom, and then boarded the rope-hauled 'man-rider' for a fourteen-minute journey towards the Swallow Wood seam face. She covered the last 400 yards in a locomotive-drawn 'man-rider', and then walked along the tailgate, the roadway leading to the end of the face, where the coal-cutting operations were explained to her. When Prince Edward was told that his mother was to inspect a mine he said, 'I bet you'll never go underground!' To prove that she did go, she took him home a lump of coal as a souvenir.

The pipeline from the first major British North Sea oilfield, the Forties, was opened by the Queen on 3rd November at British Petroleum Headquarters at Dyce, near Aberdeen. At the ceremony, which was also attended by the Prime Minister and the engineers and drillers who took part in this multi-million pound development, the Queen remarked that it was a day of outstanding significance in the history of the United Kingdom. She added, 'If we use it right this flood of energy can without doubt much improve our economic wellbeing'.

The 1975 Christmas message on television and radio broke with tradition when the Queen was shown in the grounds of Buckingham Palace, rather than in the more usual surroundings of her sitting room. She said, 'So much of the time we feel that our lives are dominated by great impersonal forces beyond our control. The scale of things and organizations seems to get bigger and more inhuman. We are horrified by brutal and senseless violence, and above all, the whole fabric of our lives is threatened by inflation, the frightening sickness of the world today'. The camera then switched to show the Queen standing on a small stone bridge by the lake, from which she threw a stone into the water. The camera picked up the ripples as she said, 'If you throw a stone into a pool, the ripples go on spreading outwards'. She continued, 'A big stone can cause waves, but even the smallest pebble changes the whole pattern of the water. Our daily actions are like those ripples, each one makes a difference, even the smallest . . .'

The National Exhibition Centre, built on a 310 acre complex near Birmingham, was opened by the Queen early in February 1976. On hearing that the completion was on time without a day lost by industrial disputes, she said, 'This is just the sort of news we all like to hear'. The new centre enables Midland industrial firms to exhibit their products without the need to travel to London.

On 27th February the Queen and Prince Philip were the guests of Fleet Street. The Queen pressed a button to set presses rolling for the lunchtime edition of the *Evening Standard* and the couple had a guided tour to see all the stages in the production of a newspaper, from the time that the reels of paper are fed into the presses, to the bundling of newspapers ready to be driven off for distribution. Before leaving, the Queen was given a copy of the newspaper with a front page picture of her arrival an hour before. 'Good gracious, that's me!', she remarked. As the Queen and Prince Philip were being shown over the foundry, the production director called over to his senior overseer, Philip Crosland, to explain the intricate process by shouting across the floor, 'Come on Philip'. 'What,' said the Queen, 'is he getting behind again?' Also that morning the couple visited the Associated Newspapers' staff of the *Daily Mail* and *Evening News*, and after lunching with the Newspaper Publishers Association, they went to the office of the *Daily Telegraph*, the *Daily Mirror* and *Sporting Life*.

THE WORK
OF A SOVEREIGN

One might be forgiven, having read this far, for assuming that the work of the Queen consists only of travelling abroad on state visits, receiving heads of state visiting Britain, participating in ceremonials, visiting various areas of Britain, and making a Christmas broadcast each year. In this book it has only been possible to pick out the major events of the reign but these represent only one aspect of the Queen's duties. Mention will now be made of her day-to-day tasks and responsibilities, the jobs we perhaps hear less about but which nevertheless represent an equally important aspect of the work of the sovereign.

Every day, for example, the Queen attends to the despatches, letters and telegrams she receives, not only from Britain but also from Commonwealth countries, much of her correspondence being from complete strangers. She sees all letters sent to her, apart from those from obvious cranks, and all have to be answered. She examines the week's cabinet minutes, the details of all cabinet meetings, and reports from the Commonwealth countries. She attends to her despatch boxes, and her paper work accompanies her wherever she goes, in Britain and abroad, even when she is at Balmoral or Sandringham, so that in a sense she never really enjoys the complete relaxation of a holiday.

The Queen entertains visiting heads of state, prime ministers and other government representatives, both foreign and from Commonwealth countries. Every time a new ambassador or minister presents to her his letters of credence, she receives him (or her) at Buckingham Palace, as she does when the high commissioner of a Commonwealth country arrives for the first time in London. The ambassador is collected from his embassy by the Marshal of the Diplomatic Corps in a state landau, and is escorted with his wife and senior staff to the Queen's presence. The Foreign Secretary introduces the diplomat to her, who then presents official letters from his government announcing his appointment and the recall of his predecessor. He presents his staff, who may be newly arrived or already known to the Queen by service under the previous ambassador. She meets these diplomats on many subsequent occasions, and has continued the annual diplomatic party started by her father, King George VI.

The Queen sees the British Prime Minister at regular intervals when Parliament is sitting, and at other times should the situation warrant it, and also sees her ministers from time to

time. Our Queen, Elizabeth II, has stored up a vast accumulation of knowledge as a result of her long continuity as sovereign, and is therefore very well informed in the affairs of state.

The Queen opens the new session of Parliament, normally in state, travelling in a carriage procession from and back to the Palace, and reading from the throne in the House of Lords the government's programme for the year. Theoretically the Queen has the right to dissolve Parliament and also to declare war, but as a constitutional sovereign she acts on the advice of her prime ministers.

The Privy Council, the oldest part of the Queen's government, is summoned at regular intervals, usually about twenty times in a year, to approve Orders in Council or perhaps to swear in new members. This generally takes place at Buckingham Palace, but can be carried out wherever the Queen may be. Though membership is for life, those who normally attend meetings are ministers (cabinet ministers are always sworn as members before taking office), and only the Accession Council is attended by a larger number of counsellors. The necessary quorum is sometimes made up by including the Queen's private secretary. The Lord President of the Council, a senior government appointment, is first admitted to the Queen to discuss the agenda and answer any questions which may arise. The counsellors are accompanied to the meetings by the Clerk of the Privy Council, a senior civil servant. Formalities are over in a few minutes, during which all remain standing. The Lord President reads the documents requiring the Queen's assent, which she approves in turn.

If the Queen is out of the country or ill, she appoints counsellors of state to perform certain duties in the United Kingdom on her behalf. Prince Philip, Queen Elizabeth the Queen Mother, and the four adult members of the royal family in seniority of succession to the throne are eligible to act. As Supreme Governor of the Church of England (she has the style of Defender of the Faith), she appoints on advice the senior churchmen, and carries out the promises she made at her Coronation. The Queen is a sincere practising member of the Church, though in Scotland she attends the services of the Church of Scotland, a Presbyterian form of worship. She also heads the legal system, and similarly makes senior appointments in England and Wales on the advice of the Lord Chancellor, and in other countries on the appropriate ministerial advice.

The Queen is the Fountain of Honour, and holds about fourteen investitures during the year. Extensive honours lists are normally published twice a year in the *London Gazette*, on New Year's Day and on the Queen's official birthday. The latter

left At the Royal Ascot meeting each year the Queen traditionally drives down the course with her guests in the state carriage drawn by four greys with two postilions.

date falls in midsummer when the sovereign's actual birthday falls elsewhere in the calendar for, in addition to the honours list, other ceremonies take place to celebrate the occasion. Honours, such as a Knighthood for a High Court Judge, a Governor or an Ambassador, are announced at the appropriate time. Certain orders of chivalry are in the Queen's personal gift, for example, the Garter and the Thistle, the Royal Victorian Order and the Order of Merit. Other honours and awards are on the recommendation of the Prime Minister of the United Kingdom, or on that of the Commonwealth countries who still sanction their bestowal. Many recipients personally receive their awards from the Queen at an investiture, although recipients of peerages do not attend investitures. These honours come into being when their patent of creation is sealed with the Great Seal. At present only life peerages are created, but it is constitutionally possible for the Queen to bestow hereditary peerages.

The Queen gives at least three garden parties at Buckingham Palace during the year, and when she is in residence at Holyroodhouse in Edinburgh, a garden party is also held there. Presentation parties have been discontinued as those who participated represented only a small minority of the population. The garden parties are consequently now much larger affairs than in the past, and invitations are sent to people from all walks of life.

There are certain events in the Queen's programme which take place annually, such as the distribution of Royal Maundy, her review of scouts at Windsor on Easter Sunday, and the Garter service in St George's Chapel Windsor which is held in June and which sometimes includes the installation of a new Knight of the Garter. On her official birthday, also in June, the Queen rides from Buckingham Palace down the Mall to take up her position at the head of her troops, the Foot Guards, at the finest military ceremonial in the year, with a history going back to about 1750. This is the Queen's birthday parade, popularly called Trooping the Colour. The birthday now takes place on a Saturday, so that London weekday traffic is not disrupted. On Remembrance Sunday the Queen takes the salute at the Cenotaph in Whitehall and, with other members of the royal family, lays a wreath in memory of the fallen in two world wars.

There are annual horse racing functions in which the Queen takes a great interest: the royal meetings at Ascot, the Derby at Epsom, and the Goodwood Races in Sussex. Other sporting occasions she attends include the Cup Final at Wembley. The Queen also enjoys Badminton, the three-day event brought into being by the Duke of Beaufort after the war, and the Horse Trials at Hickstead, Sussex, with an added interest if her daughter Princess Anne or her son-in-law Captain Mark Phillips are participating. As well as racing and horse breeding, the Queen enjoys watching her son Prince Charles play polo, and now that Prince Philip has given up this sport, she watches him carriage driving. Like her mother, the Queen is fond of dogs, keeping Corgis and Labradors.

To assist the Queen in her work she has a Household, of which the senior officer is the Lord Chamberlain. He is responsible for most of the Queen's ceremonial activities, such as royal weddings, visits, investitures and garden parties. The Private Secretary, now Sir Martin Charteris, is in constant touch with the Queen, and gives her the benefit of his assistance in all kinds of matters. The Master of the Household sees to the day-to-day arrangements in the royal palaces, and travel arrangements are the responsibility of the Master of the Horse, the Duke of Beaufort, though his deputy, the Crown Equerry, fulfils the normal arrangements. The Keeper of the Privy Purse looks after the Queen's payments. Of the Queen's ladies, the senior is the Mistress of the Robes who is present on all important occasions. The ladies-in-waiting technically are of two grades, the Ladies of the Bedchamber and Women of the Bedchamber, at least one of whom is always on duty to assist the

below *Buckingham Palace is the Queen's magnificent London home. Queen Victoria enlarged the Palace in 1846–7 to accommodate her large family by removing Marble Arch to its present site and building the East Front on the courtyard, refaced by King George V in 1911. The Palace contains offices for the Royal Household and staff.*

below *Each year the Queen walks in procession to St George's Chapel for the annual Knights of the Garter Service at Windsor Castle. Resplendently robed, the Queen's train is held by pages of honour and the royal couple are preceded and followed by officers of the most noble order.*

bottom *In an eye-catching contrast of colour the Queen poses with Her Majesty's Bodyguard of the Yeoman of the Guard. Raised by Henry VII, the bodyguard is the oldest military corps in the world.*

above left and left *Scenes of welcome in Mexico City during the Queen's visit in February 1975. Clouds of coloured paper swirl round the royal car bearing the Mexican and British flags (above left) as the party drives through the city's streets. Coloured cards held by thousands of students at a welcoming ceremony at the Zocalo, the central square (left), were turned to produce the most elaborate and effective design of the Queen.*

above *At the state banquet at the National Palace, Mexico City, guests were asked to wear national dress. Here the Queen wears the Russian Fringe tiara with a dress of leaf green georgette.*

right *In another colourful ceremony, this time in Hong Kong in April 1975, the Queen dots the eyes of a dragon to bring it to life before a traditional dragon dance performed in her honour.*

left *Prince Charles precedes the Queen in the procession through the Nave of Westminster Abbey after the ceremonial in the Henry VII Chapel when he was installed by the Queen as Great Master of the Most Honourable Order of the Bath in May 1975.*

below *Even on holiday at Balmoral the day-to-day paperwork, which accompanies the Queen in despatch boxes, has to be dealt with.*

Queen and accompany her wherever she may go.

The Queen's forebears can be traced to the earliest origin in Europe, perhaps in the world. She is not only a descendant of the English royal family, going back to Cerdic who founded the West Saxon kingdom in the sixth century, but also, through the Kings of Scots and Princes of Wales she can claim an even earlier ancestry. The Royal House of Scotland goes back to Fergus Mac Erc, who lived in the late fifth century, but the earliest line of all to be accepted by genealogists is through the Princes of Wales. Cunedda, a British warrior, who lived in the region of Hadrian's Wall during the last days of the Roman Empire, came to Wales about AD 400 to found an enduring dynasty.

In the course of the last twenty-five years the people's attitude to the monarchy has changed, and the stiff, distant for-

mality of the monarchy itself has changed with it. Through walkabouts, palace luncheons, and meetings with the people in the street, the Queen has developed a more personal contact with her subjects. The essential ceremonial, rooted in the past and unrivalled in the world, remains, but her travels and television appearances have shown her to us as a person in a modern world. Instead of staying as guests of her subjects, she and Prince Philip often spend a night or two on the royal train, which is shunted into a siding. This prevents her hosts spending large sums of money to entertain her. Similarly, while visiting Commonwealth and foreign countries, she frequently stays on board the royal yacht *Britannia* to save expenditure.

Both the Queen and Prince Philip are Commonwealth minded. The bonds that exist between Britain and the overseas Commonwealth countries are strengthened by personal ties

forged by the royal family's many visits. Previous sovereigns did not make anything like so many of these tours. Queen Victoria, for example, confined her travels to an occasional visit to Europe and consequently, as a person, she was unknown in the Empire. Edward VII, too, was far more concerned about our relations with Europe, and George V was the first to realize the Empire's importance. Almost the last word he uttered was his whisper, 'Empire?' to Lord Wigram, who reassured him, saying, 'It is all absolutely right, Sir'. War and ill health prevented King George VI from making as many Commonwealth tours as he would have liked, with the result that early in her reign the Queen became our most travelled sovereign.

Contrary to the forebodings of many, British entry into the European Economic Community has not weakened Common-

above left *Windsor Castle, Berkshire, has been the seat of our sovereign since the reign of William the Conqueror. Within the walls can be seen St George's Chapel, the Round Tower from which flies the royal standard when the Queen is in residence, and beyond the Round Tower the state apartments.*

top *The Garter Ceremony is held annually at St George's Chapel, Windsor. Founded by Edward III, the Order of the Garter is the foremost order of chivalry.*

above middle *The royal family is also able to relax at Windsor. Prince Charles chauffeurs the five-year-old Prince Edward on a go-cart.*

above *Balmoral Castle is the Queen's Scottish home in Braemar on Deeside. Here the royal couple with their two younger children take the dogs for a run.*

wealth ties, though trade with some countries inevitably has suffered; nor can the Commonwealth be written off as less important in the future to Britain than Europe.

The Commonwealth now comprises thirty-five overseas countries, including ten who acknowledge Elizabeth II as Queen, such as Canada, Australia and New Zealand. There are sovereign states, republics and monarchies who recognize her as the head of the commonwealth, and a few dependencies are still ruled from Westminster. The Second World War quickened the pace with which colonies sought independence, this being granted as soon as it was administratively possible without economic collapse. Even if achieved peacefully, as usually happened, these changes sometimes led to internal problems following the withdrawal of colonial government. Occasionally there were disputes between rival races or tribes, resulting in bloodshed, civil war or dictatorship; but it says much for the ideology of the Commonwealth that so many emerging states wished to continue their membership.

In days of the British Empire, maps of the world showed areas coloured red stretching right round the world, but when the Second World War was over these areas started to shrink. The Indian Empire, the brightest jewel in the Imperial Crown, became partitioned in 1947, before the Queen's accession. These two nations, India and Pakistan, divided into two distinct blocs, fell apart politically. When East Pakistan obtained independence as Bangladesh, this new republic elected to join the Commonwealth, but Pakistan then decided to withdraw. In South-east Asia, the Federation of Malaya obtained her independence in 1957, though the name was changed to Malaysia six years later to include Singapore, Sarawak and Sabah. Singapore, the great trading city of the east, broke away in 1965 to become a republic but, like Malaysia, elected to remain a Commonwealth member state.

Nowhere has the change during the Queen's twenty-five-year reign been more apparent than in the continent of Africa, where every country under the Queen's rule changed its constitution, as one by one of the former colonies or protectorates acquired independence. The first was the Gold Coast, to be

left and above *The Queen's love of horses is proverbial. She indulges this interest as much as possible during 'off-duty' hours, frequently visiting her horses at various studs and attending horse shows and race meetings. She is seen here (left) at the Windsor Horse Show.*

right *In contrast to the stiff formality of previous years, the style of the monarchy today has become more relaxed with the Queen developing a more personal contact with her subjects on occasions such as that shown here.*

renamed Ghana after the ancient West African kingdom of that name. Both Ghana and neighbour Nigeria, Britain's largest colony, were to become republics within the Commonwealth. Kenya, after the Mau Mau terrorist movement, achieved independence, and later became a republic, being now regarded as one of the most stable African countries. The Queen has a special regard for Kenya as the scene of her accession to the throne. The other East African states of Tanganyika, Zanzibar and Uganda also eventually adopted a republican constitution, the two former uniting to form Tanzania, and all have remained in the Commonwealth. After the break-up of the short-lived Federation of Rhodesia and Nyasaland, Rhodesia split in two, the north becoming the Republic of Zambia, while the white-dominated Southern Rhodesia retained her direct links with the Crown. Unwilling to accept British plans for majority rule the country later made its Unilateral Declaration of Independence, which is the situation to the present day. Nyasaland became the Republic of Malawi, remaining like Zambia, a Commonwealth member country.

The only major country to withdraw from the Commonwealth, apart from the Sudan, was the Union of South Africa, which after Macmillan's 'wind of change' speech, decided to become an independent republic.

The British West Indian islands all had a peaceful transition to independence, and have continued under the Queen's rule, though the Federation proved unworkable. Five of the smaller island administrations became associated states in the Commonwealth and although each is self-governing, the United Kingdom continues to be responsible for their defence and external relations.

Though different in every way from the former British Empire, the Commonwealth today may yet influence the future of the world. The most important and significant comparison one can make is this: the Empire was a collection of colonies and protectorates which formed satellites of the mother country, whereas the Commonwealth of Nations is a partnership of equal, independent countries of different races and creeds, of which the United Kingdom is one.

PHILIP
THE QUEEN'S CONSORT

Prince Philip was born a member of the Greek and Danish royal families, though he has no Greek blood. His grandfather, Prince William of Denmark, was elected King of Greece shortly after attending his sister Alexandra's wedding to the Prince of Wales, later King Edward VII. (He chose to be known as King George of Greece, since Greece shares with England the Patron Saint George.) On his assassination at Salonica in 1913, his eldest son, Constantine I, became King. Of his other sons, Prince Nicholas was the father of the late Princess Marina, Duchess of Kent, and Prince Andrew became Prince Philip's father.

Prince Andrew married Princess Alice of Battenberg in 1903 at a full-scale royal wedding attended by the Tsar and other crowned heads. (Her father, Prince Louis, became admiral of the fleet in the Royal Navy. At the outbreak of the First World War he was first sea lord, but having German blood was obliged to relinquish this post. He later anglicized his name to Mountbatten and was created Marquess of Milford Haven.)

The couple were not really compatible. Prince Andrew was a worldly man, full of fun, whereas his wife had a religious turn of mind. Later in life they parted company. Four daughters were born to them between 1905 and 1914. Then, after a long interval, an only son, Philip, was born on 10th June 1921 at 'Mon Repos', a villa on the island of Corfu built in the 1820s when the island was under British protection.

When Philip was a baby, King Constantine was forced to abdicate after the defeat of the Greeks at Smyrna in 1922, at which 40,000 troops were slaughtered. Prince Andrew, in command, was arrested, imprisoned in solitary confinement, and tried for his life. As the result of urgent appeals from King George V, the President of France and others, his life was spared, but he was banished from Greece for life. The judges' decision was not announced until the day after his trial, which was a period of great suspense for his family.

The British light cruiser *Calypso* took Prince Andrew and his family to safety, and they made their way to Paris, home of many royal exiles. Philip, then nearly eighteen months old, slept in a padded orange box in case he should fall out of the bunk. The family settled in the Rue Adolphe Ifan, and later at St Cloud, in houses belonging to Prince Andrew's brother,

Prince George of Greece. Philip attended a kindergarten at St Cloud, known by the English name of 'The Elms'.

Due to his mother's illness, much of Philip's early life was spent in England with his grandmother, the Dowager Marchioness of Milford Haven (previously Princess Louis of Battenberg), who had apartments at Kensington Palace, and with her naval son Lord Milford Haven at Lynden Manor near Maidenhead. He was sent to prep school at Cheam, but often spent long summer holidays on the Continent with his sisters, who had all married German princes in December 1930 and the following year. One of these, Princess Cecile, was tragically killed in 1937 with her husband, their two sons and his mother in an air crash. When Prince Andrew and his wife drifted apart, she stayed chiefly with her daughters and eventually went to live at Athens, where she founded the Christian Sisterhood of Martha and Mary.

Another of Prince Philip's sisters, Princess Theodora, married a son of Prince Max of Baden, the liberal-minded statesman who had given over part of his large castle, Schloss Salem, near Lake Constance to house a progressive school founded by his one-time secretary, Dr Kurt Hahn. Princess

left *Prince Philip inspects commandos at the Infantry Training Centre at Lympstone, Devon, in 1967.*
right *On his first visit to England, Prince Philip is photographed at the wedding of his Uncle Lord Louis Mountbatten (now Earl Mountbatten of Burma) to the Honourable Edwina Ashley in July 1922. He is just over a year old.*

Theodora advocated that this school would be eminently suitable for her brother, and would give their mother a chance of seeing more of him. At the age of twelve, Philip went to Salem, but within a year Dr Hahn was arrested by the rising Nazis, and was released only as the result of worldwide appeals to President Hindenburg, particularly from Ramsay Macdonald, the British Prime Minister. Philip was sent back to England, and when Hahn set up his school at Gordonstoun on the Scottish coast, Philip again became his pupil.

Prince Philip's interest in the sea and ships then began to take root. He cruised as far as Norway with the sea-scouts, and his nautical prowess led to his being allowed to sail in an open boat in the Moray Firth without adult supervision. He has been quoted as saying that he enjoyed life at Gordonstoun far more than foot-slogging at Salem. His qualities of leadership resulted in his becoming head boy or 'guardian' of the school. There is no doubt that Dr Kurt Hahn largely shaped Philip's character. 'Prince Philip's leadership qualities are most noticeable', the Doctor reported, 'though marred at times by impatience and intolerance.' He also noticed his special ease and forthrightness in dealing with all kinds of people.

Prince Philip entered Dartmouth in May 1939 as a naval cadet, a few weeks before his eighteenth birthday. Owing to Lord Milford Haven's death, the responsibility of looking after him in England passed to his younger uncle, Lord Louis Mountbatten. Philip progressed well at Dartmouth and in his first year won the King's Dirk as the best cadet of that year, and the Eardley-Howard Crockett prize as the best all-rounder. By that time the Second World War had broken out,

above *At Gordonstoun in July 1935 Philip takes part in the school's production of Macbeth.*

above right *The engagement photograph of Princess Elizabeth and Prince Philip, then Lieutenant Mountbatten R.N, taken at Buckingham Palace on 10th July 1947.*

right *In this interesting photograph taken at the Royal Dartmouth Naval College in July 1939, Philip and the thirteen-year-old Princess Elizabeth are pictured together for probably the first time. Princess Elizabeth is on the left while Prince Philip is second from the right next to Lord Mountbatten.*

far right *Princess Elizabeth is given the Freedom of the City of Edinburgh in July 1947 accompanied by her fiancé who had been granted fourteen days leave after their engagement. This was the couple's first official appearance together.*

and his uncle Lord Mountbatten, then in command of a destroyer flotilla, advised him to acquire British nationality, only to learn that the necessary 'machinery' had been suspended in wartime.

Early in 1940 Philip was posted as a midshipman to a battleship in the Mediterranean, and took part in the action off Cape Matapan in March 1941, when the Italian fleet was defeated. For his services he was awarded a mention in despatches. In 1942 he was promoted to the rank of first lieutenant. His later service included convoy duties in the North Sea, and with the British Pacific Fleet when his uncle, Lord Louis, became Supremo of South-east Asia.

Although they had met occasionally, Philip and Elizabeth first really got to know each other when he and his cousin David Mountbatten, now Lord Milford Haven, were entertained at Windsor Castle and Coppins in nearby Iver, by Elizabeth's uncle and aunt, the late Duke and Duchess of Kent (she was also Philip's cousin).

Philip was included in the Windsor Castle luncheon party to celebrate Princess Elizabeth's eighteenth birthday. When his photograph appeared on her mantlepiece, her governess, 'Crawfie' (Marion Crawford) asked her, 'Is this altogether wise? Someone might talk.' The photograph then disappeared, but a few weeks later one of a bearded naval officer appeared in its place. 'There you are!' said the Princess. 'He's incognito. I defy anyone to recognize him.'

It does not appear that Elizabeth and Philip discussed marriage until the King invited Philip to spend a month at Balmoral in the summer of 1946. As was to be expected, the press anticipated the story, and one evening paper suggested an imminent engagement, which was immediately officially

denied. Unofficially, the Prince and Princess received the King's blessing, but he insisted on continued secrecy before making a formal announcement. The King liked Philip. Both were naval men who shared a broad sense of humour, and Philip would obviously make a suitable husband for his daughter, but first there were problems to be overcome relating to Philip's naturalization as a British subject. This was now essential if they were to be allowed to marry, for he would one day be the next sovereign's consort. Although King George of Greece, again in exile as a war victim, had renounced succession to the Greek throne, there was uncertainty as to whether monarchy would be restored. King George VI's permission for the marriage might be seen either as British support for the royalist cause, or conversely as Prince Philip's abandonment of the cause. The situation was delicate.

Monarchy was restored in Greece in September 1946 by plebiscite, but so far as solving Philip's difficulty was concerned, he was told that if he abandoned Greek nationality at this time he might harm the restored royal family.

After the Balmoral visit, Philip was posted to HMS *Royal Arthur*, a naval establishment at Corsham, Wiltshire, to take a Petty Officers' course. That Christmas the King invited him to Sandringham, which naturally increased press speculation on the possible impending engagement. Although the cabinet was informed of the King's wishes, some ministers objected to Philip's nationality and to his having sisters who had all married Germans. As the King and Queen, with their two daughters, were soon to tour South Africa, the King decided that the matter had better wait until their return. They boarded the battleship *Vanguard* on 1st February. Philip was advised not to see the Princess off.

left *On their wedding day, 20th November 1947, Princess Elizabeth and Prince Philip are photographed in the Throne Room at Buckingham Palace. Norman Hartnell designed the wedding dress, a princess gown of rich ivory Duchesse satin cut on classic lines with fitted bodice, long tight sleeves and a full skirt.*

above *The happy couple on the balcony at Buckingham Palace stand with King George VI and two of the bridesmaids (Princess Margaret and Lady Mary Cambridge) on one side, and Queen Elizabeth and Queen Mary on the other.*

right *The first part of the honeymoon was spent at Broadlands, the Hampshire home of Philip's uncle and aunt, the Earl and Countess Mountbatten of Burma.*

On the trip to Cape Town, the royal family relaxed, played deck games, and danced. Princess Elizabeth was overjoyed when she heard from Philip that his naturalization had at last been successful and that he was now a British subject. There was now no bar to their engagement, and the King agreed it would be announced on their return. Philip was listed as Philip Mountbatten, a surname derived from his mother's family, as he did not possess one himself. Oldcastle, a translation of Oldenburg, a house from which his father was descended, had been rejected as too pedestrian.

Princess Elizabeth celebrated her twenty-first birthday at Cape Town. Before a grand display of fireworks and a state ball at Government House, she broadcast a message to the Commonwealth: 'I declare before you all that my whole life, whether it be long or short, shall be devoted to your service.' Three days later the tour ended and the royal family sailed for home. Again Philip was missing from the welcoming party when they arrived in mid-May.

Philip came up from Corsham to be formally interviewed by the King and Queen. At one point the King slipped out of the room with the excuse of fetching some photographs of the royal tour. Princess Elizabeth silently took his place. No announcement was then made, but the two were seen outside Buckingham Palace with linked hands, and Philip became a frequent visitor. When he could get away from the Navy, he took the Princess out in his sports car, sometimes driving down to Richmond Park in the summer evenings. Here they could walk unnoticed, she in a headscarf, and he in dark glasses.

Then, at seven o'clock in the evening on 8th July 1947, an announcement was issued to the press for publication after midnight. It read 'It is with great pleasure that the King and Queen announce the betrothal of their dearly beloved daughter the Princess Elizabeth to Lieutenant Philip Mountbatten RN, son of the late Prince Andrew of Greece, and Princess Andrew (Princess Alice of Battenberg), to which union the King has gladly given his consent.'

A small dinner party was held at Buckingham Palace in celebration. Philip went up to the Princess's sitting room beforehand, and they entered the party together, she wearing an engagement ring. This consisted of a large diamond set with smaller stones, which Philip's father had once given to his mother. The Princess exclaimed to her mother, the Queen, 'It is too big!' for there had been no opportunity to try it on first. 'We don't have to wait till it's right, do we?' she asked her father, who laughed and shook his head.

On the day of the engagement large crowds gathered in front of the Palace, singing 'All the nice girls love a sailor'. Philip was given fourteen days leave, which was spent with the royal family in Edinburgh. The couple's first official engagement was when the Princess received the Freedom of Edinburgh. Philip's face was then so unfamiliar that a caption under a press photograph had to mention that Lieutenant Mount-

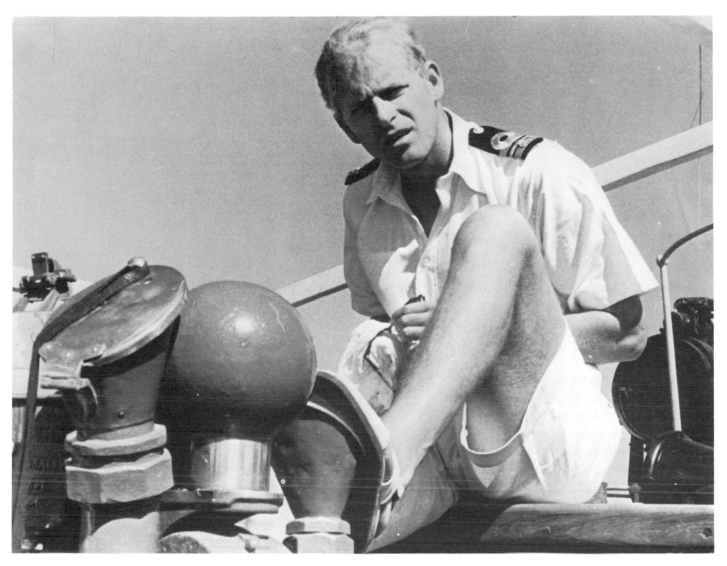

batten stood on the left, and the Lord Provost on the right.

On Philip's return to Corsham, the local public house, the Methuen Arms, gained immediate popularity as the scene of skittle matches in which he played for the Navy against the town. Some members of the team were invited to the wedding.

There was speculation as to whether the wedding would be held privately at St George's Chapel, Windsor, as had usually occurred in the past, or in full splendour in Westminster Abbey. There were precedents for an Abbey ceremony, including the marriage of the bride's parents at Westminster after the grim days of the First World War. The Princess settled matters by deciding on Westminster and this gained widespread public approval.

By the end of July the King had formally approved the marriage at a privy council meeting. By the Royal Marriages Act of 1772, no descendant of George II can contract a lawful marriage without the sovereign's consent (except in the case of Princesses who marry into foreign royal families). The date was fixed for 20th November 1947. Philip, who had been baptized in the Greek Orthodox Church, became a member of the Church of England at Lambeth Palace.

The day before Philip married, King George VI created him Duke of Edinburgh, Earl of Merioneth and Baron Greenwich, and bestowed on him the foremost order of chivalry, the Garter, which he had given to the Princess a few days earlier. He made Philip 'His Royal Highness' of the United Kingdom. None of these titles appeared on the order of the service, and the patent also did not include the word 'Prince', though how anyone could be a 'royal highness' and not *ipso facto* a Prince, was one of those conundrums which exercised constitutionalists for some years ahead. It is said that the King went to his grave without knowing that he had not formally created Philip a Prince. Philip was certainly customarily known by his title in the royal household, the press and by all and sundry. The Queen put this right in 1956 by officially creating her husband a 'Prince of the United Kingdom'.

The wedding day turned out to be a fine but dull day. Philip, suffering from a bad cold, arrived at the Abbey from Kensington Palace in good time with his best man, David Mountbatten, now Lord Milford Haven. Both wore naval uniform, the bridegroom carrying the sword which had once belonged to his maternal grandfather, Prince Louis of Battenberg. The ceremony was reported by radio. Television was in those days in its infancy, and coverage was confined to cameras positioned at the great west door to pick out the arriving company.

The King, in his uniform of admiral of the fleet, with his daughter the bride looking 'pale but composed', left Buckingham Palace at precisely sixteen minutes past eleven in the Irish State Coach of blue and gold, accompanied by the impressive sovereign's escort of Household Cavalry, wearing full dress for the first time since the War.

In the Abbey there was all the pomp surrounding the wedding of a King's daughter, but there was also the simplicity of the marriage rite. The Archbishop of Canterbury emphasized this in his address. 'In all essentials', he told the congregation of over 2,000 people, 'it was exactly the same as it would be for any cottager who might be married this afternoon in some country church in a remote village in the dales.'

The guests included the bride's grandmother, Queen Mary, looking as majestic as ever, the Kings and Queens of Denmark and Yugoslavia, the Kings of Norway, Roumania, and Iraq, the Queens of Greece and Spain, the Prince Regent of the Belgians, and many other princes and princesses. There were great commonwealth leaders, including Winston Churchill, General Smuts from South Africa, and Mackenzie King from Canada. The bridegroom's mother, Princess Alice, had for once discarded her simple nun's habit in her son's honour.

There were little moments of anxiety such as often happen at weddings. One of the pages, Prince William of Gloucester, tripped on the bride's train, and was saved from falling by Princess Margaret, the chief bridesmaid. Then, when the couple approached the altar, the bride's train became caught on the steps and the bridegroom pulled it free.

When the long bridal procession passed the King and Queen and Queen Mary, the Princess made a deep curtsey to each of them. Queen Alexandra of Yugoslavia commented that, 'One could see the muscle in Uncle Bertie's (George VI) cheek working as it always did when he was deeply moved'.

The Princess and the Duke of Edinburgh, as he had become, returned to the Palace in the Glass Coach, and soon afterwards appeared on the balcony to wave to the cheering crowds, to be joined a few minutes later by the King and Queen, Queen Mary and Princess Margaret. They came out three times in all, the bride still in her wedding dress.

After a send-off at Waterloo station, the first part of the honeymoon was spent at Broadlands, the Hampshire home of Lord and Lady Mountbatten. Although efforts had been made to ensure privacy, there were several attempts by sightseers and photographers stalking through the grounds to get a glimpse of the couple. When they arrived at Romsey Abbey on Sunday for the morning service the couple had to face vast crowds, but at Birkhall near Balmoral where they spent the rest of the honeymoon, they enjoyed seclusion at last. Meanwhile, in London, long queues passed through the state apartments of St James's Palace to see the wedding dress and the countless presents from all over the world.

The King had offered the couple Sunninghill Park near Windsor, recently purchased from the financier Philip Hill, but as the house had been occupied by the American Air Force and then by the Royal Air Force, it was in an extremely dilapidated condition. Soon after the work of renovation had started, the house was completely gutted by fire. Fortunately, the Earl of Athlone, the Princess's great uncle, offered Elizabeth and Philip the Clock House, his apartments at Kensington Palace for the duration of his stay in South Africa. This was gratefully accepted, and here the Princess and her husband

Reflecting his interest in natural history and wildlife conservation Prince Philip is shown here on a visit to the Wildfowl Trust headquarters at Slimbridge, Gloucestershire, and is being shown round by the director Sir Peter Scott.

had their first temporary home, on their return to London just before Christmas.

Clarence House, the grace and favour house adjoining St James's Palace, was made available as their London home, but, like Sunninghill, it had first to be extensively restored. Empty since the aged Duke of Connaught died in 1942, the house was extremely shabby, gas lit, and possessed only one bath. In the meantime Windlesham Moor, Surrey, was leased from Philip Hill's widow. With fifty acres of grounds, and rhododendron bushes and lakes reminiscent of Sandringham, the Moor proved an ideal setting for the beginning of the couple's happy married life.

For the first few months after marriage, Philip had a desk job in the operations division at the Admiralty; but, after a three month's staff course at Greenwich, he went back to sea as first lieutenant in HMS *Chequers*, based on Malta, where the Princess joined him as an ordinary officer's wife. Then in July 1950, Philip was promoted to lieutenant commander, and given his first command, the frigate *Magpie*. One of the crew said, 'He worked us like hell, but treated us like gentlemen'.

Philip celebrated his thirtieth birthday on 10th June 1951 on board the *Magpie*, but in the following month the King's illness brought about the end of his full-time service. He left the *Magpie* after a command of eleven months, as the 'cock ship' of the flotilla. In future he and the Princess would have to relieve the King of many of his official duties.

They now undertook a tour of America, then of Canada,

and early in 1952 were to tour East Africa, Australia and New Zealand. This of course was interrupted by the death of King George VI, as has already been described, and Philip became consort to the new reigning sovereign.

As might be expected, this event did not catch Philip entirely unprepared for his new responsibilities. When married he had read all he could find about Prince Albert, husband of the last queen regnant, Queen Victoria, and his role as prince consort, but he was disappointed to find that there is nothing laid down in the British Constitution for the position, as there is for the wife of a king. The scope of the job is a matter of personal choice. How it is done depends largely upon character, knowledge, interests, and the ways in which the consort seeks to ease the burden placed upon the Queen's shoulders.

Prince Albert summed up his experience: 'The position of the prince consort requires that the husband should entirely sink his own individual existence in that of his wife; that he should aim at no power for himself; should shun all attention, assume no separate responsibility, but make his position entirely a part of hers, fill up every gap which as a woman she would naturally leave in the exercise of her regal functions'. Basically, the situation is the same, but the methods of achieving it have vastly changed since Prince Albert's death in 1861.

In 1840 Prince Albert arrived in Britain from his father's little German Duchy of Saxe-Coburg and Gotha to marry Queen Victoria, only to find a built-in feeling of opposition to foreigners. He had no knowledge of British customs and

left *Prince Philip is also very interested in the development of science and technology and is shown here visiting the Manned Spacecraft Center at Houston in Texas during a ten-day visit to America in March 1966.*

right *A thoughtful expression from the Queen at the Badminton Horse Trials in April 1976.*

below *Prince Philip in Coweslip sails with his close friend the late Uffa Fox, during Cowes week 1968. With a love of sailing in common the two struck up a long-standing friendship and crewed together on many occasions.*

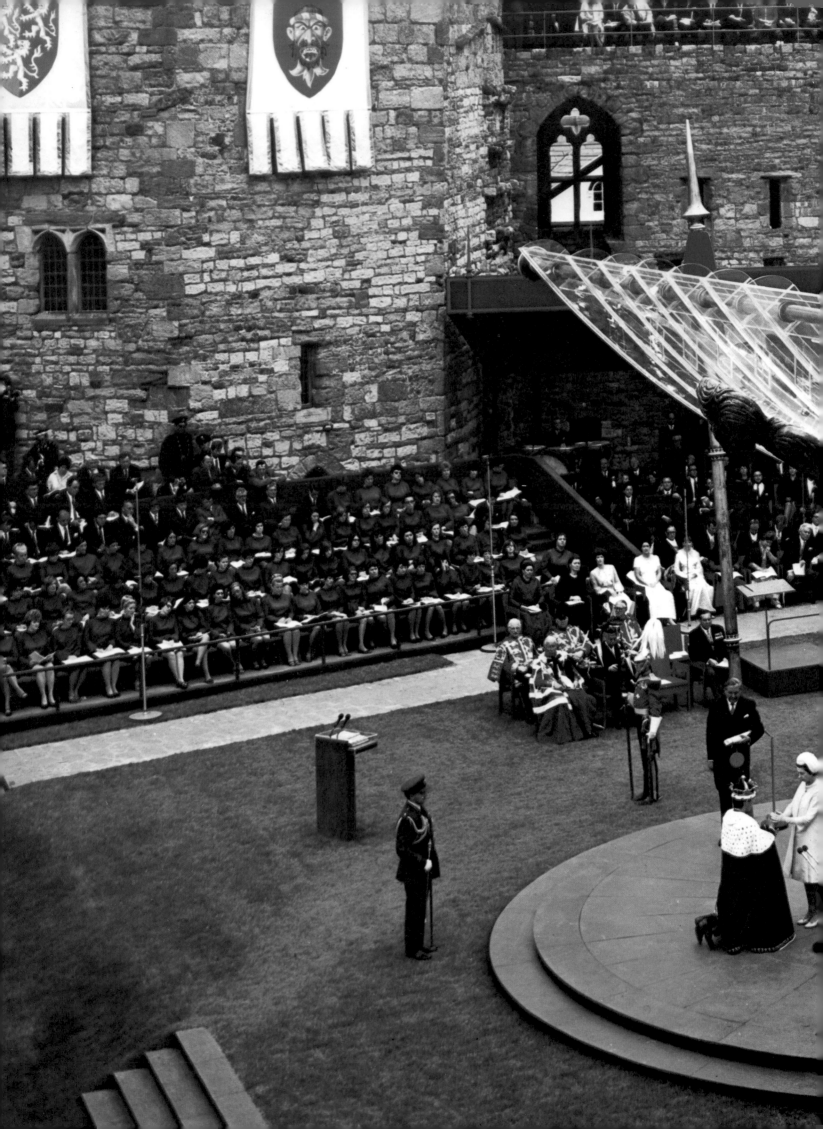

previous pages *At his investiture as twenty-first Prince of Wales at Caernarvon Castle on 1st July 1969, Prince Charles kneels before the Queen after she had placed the Coronet on his head. This ceremony, second in spectacle only to the coronation, was based largely on the 1911 investiture of the Prince of Wales, later the Duke of Windsor, but the essential ceremonial goes back to the time of the first Prince of Wales, later Edward II.*

left and below *Prince Philip relaxes. He is a gifted amateur artist (left) preferring landscapes to still life, although both figure on his canvasses. Balmoral (below) offers the chance of a spot of fly-fishing.*

character, and was unbending in many of his attitudes. On top of all this he encountered the hostility of the royal family and of much of the aristocracy.

Philip did not suffer in this way. He was brought up largely in Britain by his uncles, first by Lord Milford Haven, and then by his younger uncle, Lord Mountbatten. The Prince was the product of the British public school system, having attended Cheam and Gordonstoun (not that the latter school always followed the traditional pattern). Then, as a serving officer in the Royal Navy, his career afloat began in the hard days of the war with Germany.

Unlike Albert, Philip was not immediately placed in the position of the Queen's husband. He had just over four years of 'apprenticeship' as a member of the royal family before George VI died. During this period he was able to continue his full-time naval service until the King was taken seriously ill, and was therefore often away from home. But from the outset he showed that he would not be content to accept the role of a royal 'rubber stamp', however much that may have appealed to the royal household at the time. As his former secretary Mike Parker commented in 1970, 'With the job itself, starting from the very beginning when there was nothing at all, he had to build it up brick by brick. Apart from the King, I was surprised to find . . . that he didn't get a great deal of help . . . He had to think it out alone.'

The Prince has boundless energy and interests which run in many directions. The diversity of his knowledge has enabled him to give the greatest help to the Queen. He is now concerned with nearly 400 separate organizations, and delivers some eighty or ninety speeches a year, all of which, unless given off the cuff, he writes himself. These, delivered in a direct style, usually include a quip or two to liven up the proceedings. Often he throws calculatedly provocative remarks at his audience and if misreported is not beyond answering back, being the first member of the royal family to do so.

Foreign and Commonwealth tours have taken him all over the world. The first undertaken on his own was in 1956. He then said in Canberra: 'The Queen and I have not forgotten the wonderful time we had here three years ago. She had to stay at home this time because I'm afraid she is not quite as free as I am to do as she pleases'. Also in Australia he made a confession, 'I never managed to understand or remember your traffic rules. Luckily the police looked fairly indulgently on a naval lieutenant with a beard driving an open jeep in all the wrong places'. This displayed a sense of humour that went down well. (The regrowing of his beard echoed his naval days, even if it did not appeal to the Queen. At his homecoming party all the guests, including the Queen, donned false beards.)

Philip also makes many trips abroad to represent the organizations with which he is associated, such as that to Bulgaria in 1974 when he addressed the International Olympic Committee Congress in his capacity as president of the International Equestrian Federation. Hobbies also have led to expeditions overseas, such as his visit to the Antarctic on board the research ship *John Biscoe* in 1956. His love of natural history photography was first aroused when he bought an expensive camera for this trip to try out on the seabirds. He made his first television appearance to talk about his Antarctic experiences in a film, 'Round the World in Forty Minutes'. The talk lasted for fifty-five minutes. 'Over-time as usual', he joked afterwards. His interest in natural history brought him into contact with the World Wildlife Fund, of which he is an international trustee, as well as being president of the British National Appeal. He made a long contribution to the book *Wildlife Crisis*, which discusses threats to wildlife and conservation attitudes.

King George VI encouraged Philip to take up shooting. At first he missed as often as he hit, for his only previous experience was a little rough shooting when he was in the Navy. He particularly likes informal shooting such as the wildfowling available at Sandringham. He has reconciled his interest in wildlife conservation with shooting with the argument that far more wildlife perishes by insecticide than by the gun, but he is violently opposed to wholesale slaughter or the killing of rare species.

As soon as the Queen succeeded, Philip spent much of his time streamlining the methods by which the household was run. Here he followed the path of the Prince Consort 100 years ago, but with more drastic results. His first job was to be made warden of Windsor Great Park, which effectively gave him control over the farms on the estate. His cousin, Queen Alexandra of Yugoslavia, recalled that at a luncheon party in Windsor Castle soon afterwards there was much fun at his expense when guests suggested various designs for a suitable uniform for the post. Philip turned his office at Buckingham Palace into an operations room full of charts, with coloured stickers for his various appointments. He had the royal cars fitted with radio telephone so that he could ring up the Queen at any time when travelling, and he began to use helicopters for his visits to save time. Often he pilots his own aircraft.

The formation of the Queen's Gallery at Buckingham Palace to exhibit selections of the Queen's pictures was Philip's idea. The gallery was opened in 1952, having been converted from the bombed private chapel. Like the Queen, Philip takes a great interest in works of art, and in addition paints in oils whenever he has the time. Examples of his work, such as scenes at Sandringham, hang in guest rooms at Windsor Castle and other royal homes. The subjects include flowers, landscapes and still life, in which he benefited from tuition by the artist Edward Seago, and others. One of his works, a still life of flowers in a vase, decorates the wall of the Queen's private sitting room at Windsor. 'I don't claim any exceptional interest or knowledge or ability,' he said. 'It's strictly average'.

Industrial design was drawn to Philip's attention when the painter Edward Halliday was engaged in a portrait of him for Gordonstoun. Halliday casually mentioned that Gordon Russell was organizing a small exhibition called 'Design at Work'. This was in 1948, during the days of austerity. After they had lunched together at Halliday's club, they went along to the exhibition. Philip, immensely interested, encouraged Gordon Russell and gave him all the publicity he needed. From this start grew the Design Centre and Philip now gives annually the Duke of Edinburgh's Prize for Elegant Design. There is also a counterpart in Australia.

It seems probable that Philip's knowledge of science was first fired from his experience of the new technology of the Navy. After his election as president of the Association for the Advancement of Science for the 1951–52 session, while still serving in the Navy, he had the courage to address the largest body of top scientists ever assembled in Britain. He delivered a skilful resumé of scientific progress, its discoveries and develop-

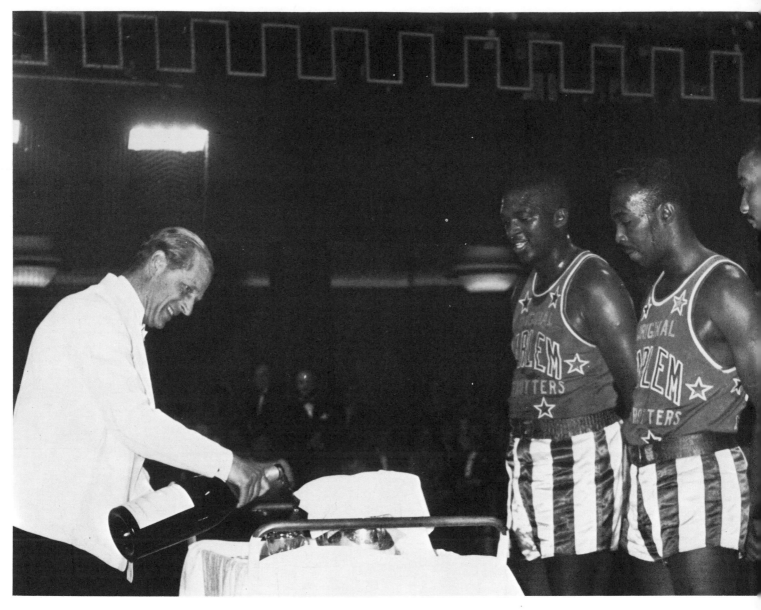

ments, and ended with his own conclusions and warnings for the future. This was his first major speech and it proved a great success.

Though technology is much to the fore these days, Philip warned, in a speech to the English-Speaking Union in 1974, that it is not one of the factors essential for civilized life. He gave the view that when the history of the second half of this century is written, it will show that people became obsessed with technology and materialism to the exclusion of all other considerations. He said that while people now enjoyed better health and greater material comfort than ever before, the standards of civilization, as measured by personal, group and international relationships, certainly had not improved.

Prince Philip takes an interest in and has visited the Royal Aeronautical Establishment at Farnborough, the Atomic Research Centre at Harwell, the Chemical Research Laboratory at Teddington, and other scientific establishments. The Commonwealth too, claims his attention. In October 1974, for example, he presided at the AGM of the Australian Conservation Foundation, held at the Australian Academy of Science.

The heritage of the past and conservation in the future are subjects in which Prince Philip has specialized. In 1972 he

was busy with the World Conservation Year. Three years later, as president of the UK Council of the European Heritage Year, he took part in the final Thames Television programme on European Historic Houses, giving his views on their future in these days of high taxation. Another aspect in which he is deeply interested is the preservation of historically important ships, which are often suffering badly from neglect in remote harbours. Money is the first priority for this conservation activity and to this end he set up the Maritime Trust.

As a fund raiser Philip is in his element. He gets much fun out of the Variety Club of Great Britain and in his position as patron and twelfth man of the Lords Taverners, who are mainly cricket-loving actors. Though the press is often more concerned with the high jinks at the events of these two organizations, the end product of money raised is, of course, the principal objective.

Prince Philip has done much in the cause of youth, such as his involvement with the Playing Fields Association, of which he has been a hard-working president ever since his uncle Lord Mountbatten stood down in 1949. This association, which celebrated its Golden Jubilee Year in 1975, was founded by his father-in-law King George VI when Duke of York, then known as the 'Industrial Prince' from his activities in

left *As patron and twelfth man of the Lords Taverners Cricket team, Prince Philip is often involved in their fund raising activities. Here he pours champagne for the Harlem Globetrotters during their basketball match against a Lords Taverners team during the Annual Ball at Grosvenor House, London, in November 1963.*

right *Prince Philip meets three young motorcyclists at the Young Volunteer Force Headquarters, Wolverhampton, who proudly showed him the wall of a nearby house which they had plastered. The Duke was apparently impressed by the array of badges displayed by the trio, saying, 'You've got more medals than me!'*

business welfare. The association stresses the importance of children having somewhere to play, as well as giving advice to local authorities and other groups such as voluntary bodies. Money is needed to put these schemes into action, and this is where fund raising becomes an important activity.

When Philip became president, he told his committee: 'Gentlemen, I want to assure you that I have no intention of being a sitting tenant in this post'. Initially he made it a full-time office job, studying their accounts, suggesting improvements in methods, and even licking envelopes for appeals. When a Silver Jubilee Fund was launched with a target of half a million pounds, he told the members, 'If you can raise a million, I can soon show you how to spend it'.

In 1956, Philip instituted the Duke of Edinburgh's Award scheme as a challenge for young people to reach certain standards in their activities outside their schools or jobs. The DEA soon became popular, and spread throughout the commonwealth. For prowess in the 400 types of activities which qualify for entry, bronze, silver and gold medals are awarded. Sustained effort and perseverance are looked for in those who make the best of their abilities, since candidates are not competing with each other. Those who are awarded gold medals are invited to Buckingham Palace to meet Prince Philip.

Philip's love of sailing in racing ships and boats dates back to his Gordonstoun days and the Navy. As a Dartmouth cadet he had a chance of sailing anything from a twelve-and-a-half-foot Dart one-design dinghy, to the thirty-seven ton yawl *Amaryllis*. He enjoyed regular yacht racing at Cowes from the time he and the Queen were given *Bluebottle*, a Dragon class yacht, by the Island Sailing Club of Cowes, as a wedding present. His old friend, the late Uffa Fox, well-known as a boat builder, was a long-standing sailing companion. When Prince Charles and Princess Anne were young he took them sailing in Scottish lochs; and when Philip owned the ocean-going yawl, *Bloodhound* (sold in 1969), they explored the west coast of Scotland together. After Cowes regatta week Philip likes to sail northwards to Scotland for the royal family's summer holiday at Balmoral.

Philip was introduced to polo early in life by that great player, his uncle, Lord Mountbatten. When he and the Queen moved into Buckingham Palace he rigged up the gymnasium with an electric horse and padded wall, against which he slammed shots with his polo stick. Becoming an accomplished and hard rider, he gave no quarter and expected none, and was not afraid of tumbles. Polo was stimulating exercise which kept him fit and enabled him to get rid of his surplus energy.

On reaching the age of fifty, and after having had trouble from a wrist injury, Philip gave up playing at the end of the 1971 season, though he still occasionally umpires. Instead, he took up carriage driving, which was then undergoing a revival in Britain, and by popularizing the sport he has helped to raise its status to Olympic standards.

Though he takes an interest in ponies in addition to polo, Philip's love of horses does not fall into the same category as that of the Queen and their two elder children. Unlike her, he has taken little interest in racing or horse breeding.

His direct, sometimes blunt approach, and occasional sudden irritation, have caused quarrels with both pressmen and photographers, though he insists that it is not their work to which he objects, but their intrusion of privacy and the misrepresentation of the royal family in the press. On one occasion, for example, he was alleged to have soaked some photographers at the Chelsea Flower Show. From time to time we read headlines in the press, such as, 'Philip Raps Press Again' in the *Daily Express*, 'Philip Starts Storm' in the *Daily Mail*, and 'MPs Say Censure Prince' in the *Sunday Telegraph*, which keep him in the news.

More than anything else, Prince Philip regretted that his active naval service ended with the King's illness. He is not sorry that he went straight from school to Dartmouth and the Navy. 'I am not a graduate of any university,' he once said. 'I am not a humanist or a scientist, and oddly enough, I don't regret it. I owe my allegiance to another of the world's few great fraternities, the fraternity of the sea.'

Philip's task is to help the Queen modernize the monarchy, but without any loss of its mystique or its heritage from the past. Certain events which had outlived their usefulness such as presentation parties had to go. Philip had a hand in this as he probably had with the introduction of 'walkabouts', and the introduction of informal luncheon parties at Buckingham Palace.

Thirsty Prince Philip downs a quick pint at the Tunnel House Inn, near Cirencester, Gloucestershire, in July 1975, during the National Carriage Championships. Forced to give up polo in 1971 due to recurring trouble from an early wrist injury, the Duke is now an enthusiastic carriage driver.

133

THE ROYAL CHILDREN

CHARLES

Prince Charles, the Prince of Wales, was born at Buckingham Palace on 14th November 1948, when Clarence House was being converted as a home for his parents. It was the first birth at the Palace for over sixty-two years, the last being that of Princess Patricia, daughter of a former occupant of Clarence House, the Duke of Connaught. It was also the first royal birth since at least Stuart times that had not been witnessed by the Home Secretary. Some believe this custom dates from 1688 when James II's son, Prince James Edward, was alleged, without foundation, to have been smuggled into St James's Palace in a warming pan, while others consider it has an earlier origin. King George VI decided that it was unnecessary to retain the practice.

Though born with a royal title, it was only five days before Charles was born that letters patent declared that any children of Princess Elizabeth and the Duke of Edinburgh were to be princes and princesses. If this had not been decreed they would have taken their rank from their father, like the children of other Dukes. Charles, the eldest son, would have been known as Earl of Merioneth, and Anne would have become Lady Anne Mountbatten.

Charles proved a shy boy, but always conscious of the feelings of others. When he was only three years old his grandfather, the King, died, and Charles told his grandmother, 'Don't cry, Grannie,' patting her hand. His position changed radically as heir apparent to the throne, for as soon as his mother became Queen he automatically became Duke of Cornwall, with a string of other peerages.

In the following year, Prince Charles witnessed his mother's coronation from the royal box in Westminster Abbey, sitting between the Queen Mother and Princess Margaret. 'Grannie, isn't it nice?' he whispered, though when his mother emerged from being annointed in a simple white gown after the previous magnificence, he looked startled and worried. The Queen reassured him with a little smile, which onlookers noticed as her only one throughout the long ceremonial.

Charles' education started when he was five years of age. Miss Catherine Peebles, soon to be known as Miss P, or Mispy, who had been Prince Michael's governess, came to give him grounding in reading and writing, which he liked, arithmetic, geography and history, later adding French to his lessons. Then, at the age of eight, he went to a small school, Hill House, in Hans Place, London, where he spent two terms, playing his first organized game of football on the Duke of York's Headquarter Grounds at Chelsea. He was then ready to go as a boarder to his father's old preparatory school at Cheam, near Newbury, Berkshire, where his parents took him in September 1957. At the end of the first term he was summed up as 'still a little shy, but very popular; passionately keen on and progressing at games; academically a good scholar'. A boy there called him 'a jolly decent ordinary sort of chap', and his headmaster summed him up as 'a very good mixer'.

While at Cheam, Prince Charles was created Prince of Wales and Earl of Chester. These titles are not held automatically by the heir apparent, but it is customary to bestow them soon afterwards. In this case the Queen did not wish to give them to Prince Charles until he was old enough to understand something about the Principality of Wales. It was intended that the Queen and Prince Philip should tour Wales, where she would make the announcement at the closing ceremony of the sixth British and Commonwealth Games in Cardiff Arms Park on 26th July 1958. Unfortunately, when the day arrived, the Queen had a heavy cold which developed into sinusitis, and her medical advisers recommended that she should stay indoors. A recording of her speech was rushed to Cardiff, where it was introduced by Prince Philip. 'By a cruel stroke of fate,' she said, 'I have been prevented from visiting North and South Wales and seeing something of the British and Commonwealth Games . . .' She concluded with these words,

left *The christening of Prince Charles at Buckingham Palace on 15th December 1948. The infant Prince is wearing the robe of Honiton lace first used by Queen Victoria's children.*
right *Charles at three years of age takes an active interest in his baby sister Anne at Clarence house.*

above *Charles at eleven years of age in a family scene at Balmoral with Princess Anne and the baby Prince Andrew.*

left *On his first day at Gordonstoun in May 1962, and accompanied by his father, an old boy, Charles is shown around by Captain Iain Tennant of the Board of Governors.*

above right *On a six-month exchange trip to Timbertop in the Australian outback in 1966, Charles enjoyed a varied programme of strenuous outdoor activities. Here he is shown using a fire hose.*

far right *Continuing his education at Cambridge, Charles featured in fourteen sketches of the revue at Trinity College in February 1969.*

'I have therefore, decided to mark it (this occasion) further by by an act which will, I hope, give as much pleasure to all Welshmen as it does to me. I intend to create my son Charles Prince of Wales today. When he is grown up I will present him to you at Caernarvon.' The crowd of 36,000 people roared their delight at having once more a Prince, the twenty-first possessor of the title, and burst into singing 'God Bless the Prince of Wales', an anthem that had not been heard since Wales had last had a Prince, twenty-two years before.

Charles automatically became a Knight of the Garter, for on its foundation by King Edward III, the Prince of Wales became a constituent part of this great order of chivalry. The nine-and-a-half-year-old Prince, one of the few who had been let into the secret, heard his mother's broadcast by radio from the headmaster's study.

At the age of thirteen, Charles followed in his father's footsteps once more by entering Gordonstoun, a decision which was not taken lightly. Certain other schools such as Eton were considered, but the Prince himself was consulted and Gordonstoun it was. This choice proved a great challenge for him, for inevitably comparisons with his father were made throughout his education. The school, known for its dedication to the principles of leadership, team spirit and consideration for others, gave him the self-confidence he needed. His own behaviour and willingness to conform overcame any difficulty there might have been over his acceptance by the other boys. He suffered from press publicity, of which the cherry brandy episode is only one example. When engaged on a marine exercise aboard the yacht *Pinta* Charles and the rest of the party

berthed at Stornaway in the Outer Hebrides, and went ashore to the local hotel. Here the fourteen-year-old Prince was spotted drinking and press accounts were soon plastered over front pages, although the whole story soon came into perspective as a boyish prank. On another occasion, some of his essays in his green exercise book were stolen, to be published in facsimile by certain magazines on the continent.

At Gordonstoun Charles developed his love of music. He played the cello, trumpet and guitar, and was given full rein during his holidays at Windsor Castle, when the Queen allowed him and his sister to use a room in the Victoria Tower for music and record playing.

He was seventeen when he flew out to Australia to Timbertop on an exchange system, a Geelong boy, David Manton, taking his place at Gordonstoun. Charles spent two terms at Timbertop, the outback section of Geelong Grammar School, near Melbourne, which had impressed the Queen on a previous visit. He arrived at the end of January, 1966 and took up residence in one of the school's eight huts. Geelong boys spend their fourth year at Timbertop, where they do everything themselves. The only domestic staff at the school is the cook. This was a period of hard physical work for Charles: chopping wood; cross-country runs through the bush; climbing peaks and cleaning out fly traps; as well as doing ordinary school work.

Weekends were usually spent hiking, and there were trips further afield, such as to New Guinea, which made a great impression on the young Prince. After six months of this toughening-up programme, which he greatly enjoyed, Charles flew

far left and left *Prince Charles passes out from the Royal Naval College, Dartmouth, in October 1971, and chats with chief petty officers in the mess.*

below left *Helicopter pilot training at the Royal Naval Air Station, Yeovilton, in October 1972.*

right *Taking navigation bearings on the bridge wing of* HMS Minerva *off the West Indies in March 1973.*
below right *The 'Tarzan' commando assault course at the Royal Marine Training Centre, Lympstone in Devon, includes stream-wading.*

off to Mexico en route to Jamaica, where he joined his father and Princess Anne at the Commonwealth Games.

On his return to Gordonstoun, Charles was appointed head of his house and guardian of the school. He became the proud owner of a silver medal of the Duke of Edinburgh's Award Scheme for initiative during an expedition in the Cairngorms, and for his achievements in athletics, pottery and first-aid.

In October 1967 Prince Charles arrived at Trinity College, Cambridge, to read archaeology and anthropology. Despite several absences to carry out duties of state, he still managed to put in more work than most of his fellow undergraduates. He also spent a term away from Cambridge at the University College of Wales, Aberystwyth, immediately prior to his investiture as Prince of Wales, principally to study the Welsh language. In addition to his hard work at Trinity he managed to play polo (the captain of the Cambridge team called him the best player there), join in debates at the Cambridge Union, practice the cello and participate in other activities. In his last year he appeared in fourteen sketches in the annual Trinity revue. After a happy period of three years he gained a second class Bachelor of Arts degree in history, and later received his Master of Arts degree.

While still an undergraduate, his plans for a career in the Royal Navy were announced. 'I am looking forward to it very much,' he said, and, 'I hope I shall not be too seasick.' Before joining the senior service, however, he was accepted as one of the Graduate Entry One Group at the Royal Air Force College, Cranwell, having qualified for a private pilot's licence at the age of twenty-one. At Cranwell he flew 400 mph jets, Phantom bombers and new Nimrod anti-submarine jets as a copilot, and became the first heir apparent to make a parachute descent. After obtaining his wings Charles went to Dartmouth in mid-September 1971 to study at the Royal Naval College, preparatory to his time at sea. After his training in seamanship, navigation and other naval duties, he attended a three-month course of helicopter training at the Royal Navy Air Station, Yeovilton, Somerset. He completed 105 flying hours in 45 days, '. . . quite a hard flying rate', and was awarded the Double Diamond Trophy for the student who had made the most progress. He

took the tough commando-training assault course at the Royal Marines Training Centre at Lympstone, Devon, in his stride. The endurance and 'Tarzan' course he called 'a most horrifying expedition'. He had to swing over chasms on ropes, slide down the ropes at death-defying speeds, and then walk across wires and climb up rope ladders strung between a pool and a tree. When talking with the News Editor of the *Evening Standard* on 7th February 1975, he was asked which aspect of his naval career he enjoyed most. 'I adore flying, and I personally can't think of a better combination than naval flying— being at sea and being able to fly. I think that people who fly in the Fleet Air Arm are of a very high standard . . . These people are taking all kinds of risks. Taking off and landing on carriers, particularly at night, is no joke at all . . .' He took over his first naval command, the minehunter *Bronington*, 360 tons, at Rosyth Dockyard on 9th February 1976. The ship has a crew of 5 officers and 34 men and is known throughout the fleet as 'old quarter-past-eleven' because of her pennant number of 1115. *Bronington* is mainly engaged in mine counter-measure exercises – the location of mines on the sea bed and their disposal by divers.

In 1969, the year of his investiture, the Prince became colonel-in-chief of the Royal Regiment of Wales, and in 1975 took over as colonel of the Welsh Guards from his father, who had held the appointment for nearly twenty-two years. In his farewell address, Prince Philip said, 'My son is the only person to whom I would willingly hand over'.

One of Prince Charles' earliest ceremonial functions was his installation in June 1968 as a Knight of the Garter in St George's Chapel, Windsor. He attended his first Privy Council meeting in April 1970, and in that year was also introduced to the House of Lords. He made his maiden speech on 13th June 1974, on sports and leisure, this being the first time a member of the royal family had spoken there for about 100 years. 'The fact that I am making, with some trepidation, my maiden speech must indicate that we have a problem over recreation,' he told his fellow peers. He spoke again in the House of Lords a year later, on voluntary service to the community, '. . . which,' said the Bishop of Leicester, 'brought a breath of sea and mountain air to invigorate us on this summer afternoon'.

But the most splendid ceremonial Charles has ever undertaken was undoubtedly his investiture as Prince of Wales in Caernarvon Castle on 1st July 1969, which, despite various threats from nationalists, passed without incident. Since then

far left *Other features of the 'Tarzan' course are ropewalks, scaling walls and crawling through half-submerged pipes, all taken in his stride by Charles.*

below left *On a tour of the North West Territories of Canada in April 1975, Prince Charles tries his hand at snowmobile driving in the Arctic at Pangnirtung.*

below *Service training included participation in hockey matches.*

right *Polo is a more familiar sport for Prince Charles and under the expert tuition of his father he rose to be a team captain in 1972, leading the home side on a Young England versus Young America match at Smith's Lawn, Windsor.*

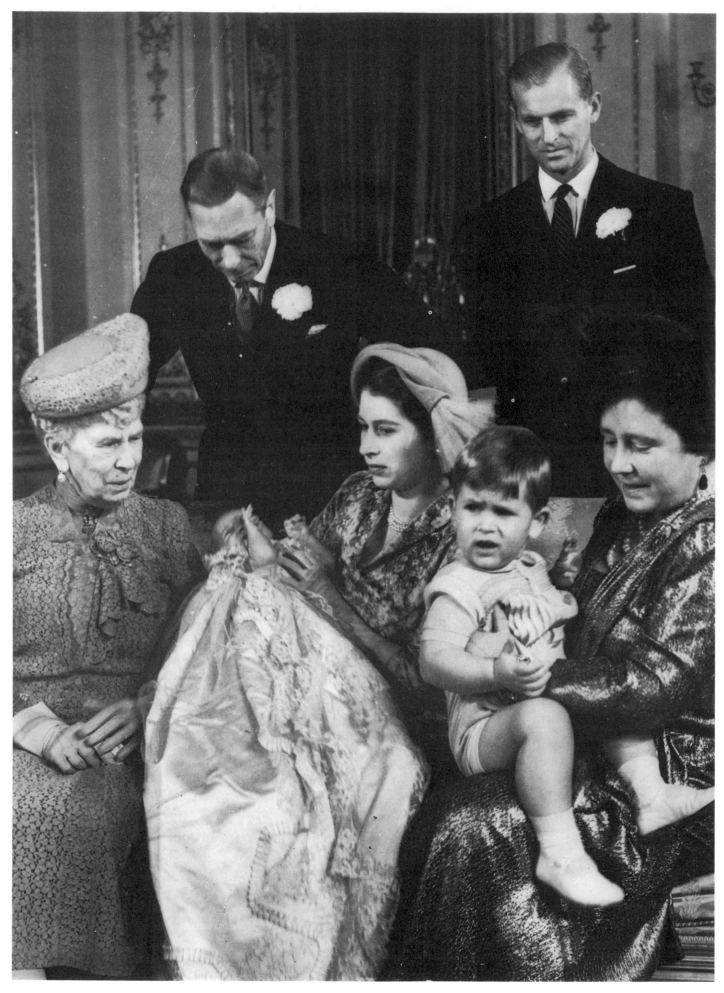

left *Princess Anne's christening group at Buckingham Palace on 21st October 1950. Anne is wrapped in the robe worn by Charles at his christening (see page 134). Queen Elizabeth holds Charles on her knee while King George VI and the proud great-grandmother Queen Mary look on.*

right and below *Two happy family scenes at Balmoral in September 1955, with Anne and Charles aged five and six respectively.*

he has taken on more and more duties in Wales.

Another area with which he is vitally concerned is the Duchy of Cornwall, some of whose properties lie outside that county.

On 28th May 1975 the Queen installed her son as Great Master of the Order of the Bath, in Henry VII's Chapel, Westminster Abbey. With the other Knights Grand Cross, in their mantles of crimson satin lined with white taffeta, he looked an impressive figure. For this occasion he shaved off the beard he had previously grown, but retained the moustache.

One visit overseas which the Prince enjoyed more than most was his tour of Canada in April 1975 when he travelled to the frozen Territories of the north. In Resolute Bay he dived for half-an-hour below the five-foot thick Arctic ice, wearing a special rubber suit with hot air circulation inside. An official commented at the time that 'The water was so darned cold that in an ordinary diver's wet suit he would be dead in three minutes.' This hair-raising feat came about because Charles had expressed an interest in the under-the-ice experiments of scientists.

Charles thoroughly enjoys the Australian way of life, and in October 1974 made his second visit there in the course of a year, flying from Fiji. After his speech at the New South Wales Parliament at Sydney to mark the 150th anniversary of that state, the *Melbourne Herald* announced enthusiastically that he would probably be Australia's next Governor-General, but even if asked, it is probable that he would not be available for

above left Her interest in horses encouraged from an early age by her mother, Princess Anne here adjusts the bridle of one of her ponies at Balmoral.

left First day introductions at Benenden School, Kent, at the start of term in September 1963. The Queen talks to the headmistress while Anne meets her housemistress.

right A keen polo player, Prince Charles takes a well-earned breather during a match on Smith's lawn, Windsor Great Park, at the Guards' Polo Club.

top *A fine study of the Queen's second son, Prince Andrew, taken in April 1976.*

above *In boisterous, carefree mood, Prince Charles plays with his cousin Lady Sarah Armstrong-Jones at Balmoral in November 1972.*

left *On a Balmoral picnic, outings much enjoyed by the royal family, Prince Philip and Princess Anne barbecue sausages and steaks during the summer of 1972.*

overleaf *Norman Parkinson's engagement photograph of Princess Anne and her fiancé Captain Mark Phillips, taken in the Long Gallery at Windsor Castle a few weeks before their wedding in November 1973.*

some years to come. He has also visited many other Commonwealth countries, including New Zealand, both on royal tours and on his naval service.

Prince Charles has proved to be a conscientious and hard-working Prince, with a sense of humour. His feelings were well expressed in 1975 when his grandmother the Queen Mother conferred upon him an honorary Doctorate of Law at London University. Attacking those pessimists who do us ill-service, he said, 'We are a great nation of self-deprecators. We are having a field-day at the moment. We must retain our sense of humour and ability to laugh at ourselves.'

ANNE

Princess Anne, the Queen and Prince Philip's only daughter and second child, was born on 15th August 1950 at Clarence House, the only one of their four children to have been born there. Near in age to her elder brother Prince Charles, there has always been a close bond between them. Anne and Charles were looked after by capable nannies, Helen Lightbody and Mabel Anderson, and Anne, an attractive, flaxen-haired baby, soon showed her strong will and tomboy character. The move from Clarence House took place soon after her mother became Queen, when Anne was eighteen months old.

At the age of five, Anne started her lessons at Buckingham Palace with her governess, Miss Peebles. Early in life she developed a love of riding, and before she was three years old she received her first lessons from her mother. Later Sybil Smith, who ran a riding school near Windsor, gave her and Prince Charles regular tuition and the two joined the Garth Pony Club in Berkshire.

Life was lonely for Princess Anne after her brother went to school, and when she reached the age of thirteen her parents wisely decided to send her to boarding school, choosing Benenden in Kent. The Queen took her there at the beginning of the autumn term of 1963, and Anne became one of their 300 pupils. Her scholastic life included weekly riding lessons, and as soon as she was qualified, she entered pony club trials and events.

Anne left Benenden in the summer of 1968. Alison Oliver, whose husband Alan is well-known in show-jumping circles, then began to give Anne valuable assistance in her riding programme and eventing. Her stables at Brookfield Farm are not far from Windsor, and instructor and pupil have been firm friends ever since they met.

Anne performed her first solo engagement on St David's Day 1st March 1969, when she presented leeks to the Welsh Guards on a bitterly cold parade ground at Pirbright, Surrey. In May of that year she took part in the state visit of her parents to Austria, although she missed the first two days with a bout of 'flu. She was, however, able to join in some of the events, including a practice ride at the famous Spanish Riding School in Vienna. Anne travelled with her parents on their Commonwealth Tour in the spring of 1970 and, as well as

above right *Expressions of concentration in evidence as fifteen year old Princess Anne receives photography instructions from her mother.*

right *In Georgian nobleman's costume, Anne takes* Feudal Knight *through the complicated routine of the quadrille at the Benenden Church Fete in July 1969.*

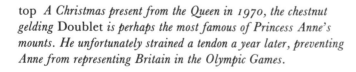

top *A Christmas present from the Queen in 1970, the chestnut gelding* Doublet *is perhaps the most famous of Princess Anne's mounts. He unfortunately strained a tendon a year later, preventing Anne from representing Britain in the Olympic Games.*

middle and above *In one of the boldly designed hats for which she has become noted, Anne is seen here on a formal occasion at Torpoint in May 1972, and more informally dressed watching and enjoying naval seamanship training.*

above *On the occasion of Princess Anne's marriage to Captain Mark Phillips on 14th November 1973, the wedding group gather at Buckingham Palace for an official photograph. Identified in the key are the following:*
1 Princess Beatrice of the Netherlands. 2 Princess Alice, Countess of Athlone. 3 James Ogilvy. 4 Prince Edward. 5 Lady Sarah Armstrong-Jones. 6 Marina Ogilvy. 7 Lady Helen Windsor and 8 Lord Nicholas Windsor, children of the Duke and Duchess of Kent. 9 Earl of St Andrews. 10 King Constantine of Greece. 11 Queen Anne-Marie of Greece. 12 Crown Prince (Harald) of Norway. 13 Crown Princess (Sonja) of Norway. 14 Captain Mark Phillips. 15 Princess Anne. 16 The Queen. 17 The Queen Mother. 18 Princess Margaret. 19 Viscount Linley. 20 Lord Snowdon. 21 Prince Michael of Kent. 22 Major Peter Phillips. 23 Mrs Peter

Phillips. 24 *Duchess of Kent.* 25 *Captain Eric Grounds (best man).* 26 *Prince Philip.* 27 *Duchess of Gloucester.* 28 *Princess Alice, Duchess of Gloucester.* 29 *Prince of Wales.* 30 *Princess Sophie of Spain (now Queen).* 31 *Prince Andrew.* 32 *Prince Juan Carlos (now King of Spain).* 33 *Princess Alexandra.* 34 *Hon. Angus Ogilvy.* 35 *Duke of Gloucester.* 36 *Lord Mountbatten of Burma.* 37 *Sarah Phillips.* 38 *Prince Claus of Netherlands.* 39 *Duke of Kent.*

fulfilling a round of public engagements, she managed when in Australia to fly on a two-day private visit to the Talbarea sheep-station at Cunnamulla.

Like her father, Princess Anne is keenly interested in photographing wild life. The children's television programme 'Blue Peter' has twice screened the films she shot in Kenya in February 1971, on behalf of the Save the Children Fund, of which Anne is their hard-working President. When she and her father represented the Queen at the magnificent celebrations at Tehran that October, given by the Shah of Iran, she took the opportunity of riding a three-year old stallion called *Belderchine* and her horsemanship much impressed the Iranians.

In October of the following year Anne accompanied the Queen and Prince Philip to Yugoslavia on their state visit to President Tito, the royal family's first visit to a communist country. Anne delighted the crowds by wearing one of the hats for which she has become famous, this time of a conical, medieval design. In the same year she was on safari in Ethiopia, where she took a three-day trip in the mountains, much of it by mule.

Princess Anne has three Army appointments. She is colonel-in-chief of the 14th/20th Hussars, the Worcestershire and Sherwood Foresters, both of whom she has visited in Germany, and of the 8th Canadian Hussars. She is also commandant-in-chief of the Ambulance and Nursing Cadets of the St John's Ambulance Brigade, being 'in charge' not only of British cadets but also of those of the Commonwealth, and is the enthusiastic patron of the Riding for the Disabled Association.

For her twenty-first birthday the 14th/20th Hussars gave Princess Anne a car registration plate bearing the number and initial of the Regiment, 1420 H, which they had discovered on a milk float. Above this plate she fixed the regimental badge, a Prussian eagle, on her Scimitar car.

Perhaps the most significant occasion in Princess Anne's riding career came when the Queen made her a birthday present of the chestnut colt, *Doublet*, which had been bred from her own stables. On this favourite mount the Princess competed in many three-day championships, becoming not only European Champion in 1971, when competing at Burghley, but also being voted Sportswoman of the Year by the Sports Writers' Association, and BBC Sports Personality of the Year.

Anne first met Mark Phillips in 1968 at a party given for the equestrian team at the Mexico Olympics in 1968, when he was the reserve rider for the British three-day event team and she a spectator. It was not until the Munich Olympics in 1972 however, that they became close friends. By the autumn of that year the friendship had ceased to be secret. Despite a Buckingham Palace statement on 2nd March 1973 that they were no more than good friends, with a mutual love of horses, it was later learned that they had become secretly engaged that Easter.

Mark Phillips was a lieutenant serving with the Queen's Dragoon Guards, living at Great Somerford, the Wiltshire home of his parents, where Anne became a frequent visitor. His love of horses also goes back to his early days, and he rides whenever it is possible for him to fit this in with his military duties. He has become one of the country's leading three-day event riders, and in 1970 at Punchestown, County Kildare, for

A delightfully happy photograph of Princess Anne and her husband enjoying a joke at the Badminton Horse Trials in April 1974.

153

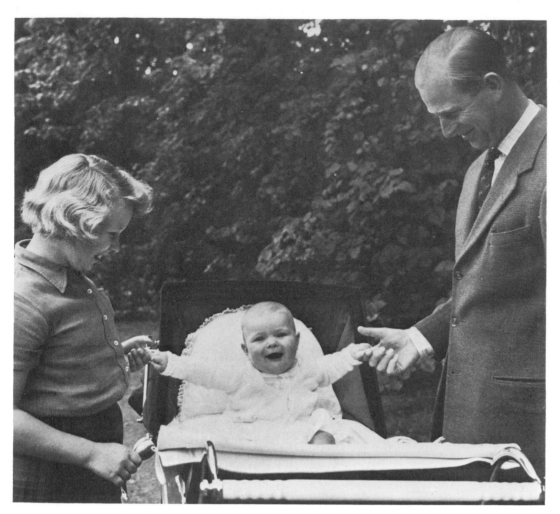

left *The baby Prince Andrew, born on 19th February 1960, proudly grasps the hands of his father Prince Philip and his sister Princess Anne at Balmoral in the summer of that year.*

below *Again at Balmoral, Prince Andrew, now six years old, lets go the lead of the corgi puppy* Tiny *who promptly raced off after the Queen about to inspect a guard of honour.*

right *Andrew at fifteen years of age prepares to take off with his gliding instructor to complete his initial training as a glider pilot. He is the third member of the royal family to receive flying training from the Royal Air Force, but the first to display wings as a glider pilot.*

example, he helped to win the World Championship for Britain. In the two following years he achieved a sensational double by winning the Badminton Horse Trials, both times riding his dark bay gelding, *Great Ovation*. To foil the press and cameramen who continually followed them about, Anne and Mark occasionally had to resort to travelling in a horsebox.

The news of Anne's engagement was announced when all the royal family were holidaying at Balmoral. Major Derek Allhusen, leader of the three-day event team at the Mexico Olympics commented, 'They are admirably suited, and the Princess couldn't have met a nicer person than Mark'. The Queen, highly delighted at the impending match, formally gave her consent to the marriage at a Privy Council Meeting at Buckingham Palace on 24th July. By then, Mark Phillips had achieved his promotion to Captain. The wedding took place in splendour in Westminster Abbey on Wednesday 14th November 1973.

Early in the new year 1974, Princess Anne and her husband moved into their first home, Oak Grove at Sandhurst in Berkshire, on his appointment as an instructor at the Royal Military Academy there. On the 20th March Anne and Mark, with Anne's lady-in-waiting, Miss Rowena Brassey, drove to the city to watch a documentary film called 'Riding Towards Freedom', being shown by the Riding for the Disabled Association. Nearing Buckingham Palace on their return, their car was held up by a gunman in the Mall. Fortunately despite shooting and threats of violence, the party was unharmed, but some of those who challenged the attacker, including police officers, were shot. The Princess visited the victims in hospital,

and later the Queen gave them awards for bravery.

Princess Anne is eligible for the title of Princess Royal, which has previously been conferred for life on the eldest or only daughter of a sovereign in a vacancy, but so far this has not been granted to her. It has been said that as that last Princess Royal, King George V's only daughter Princess Mary, was 67 on her death in 1965, the title is more suited to an older woman.

ANDREW AND EDWARD

Prince Andrew was born in 1960, shortly after the Queen celebrated the eighth anniversary of her accession. There was a rumour that the child was expected on St Valentine's Day, 14th February, but he arrived in the late afternoon of Friday the 19th. The day before, Prince Philip apologized at a Guildhall luncheon for his wife's absence. 'As you realize,' he said, 'she has other matters to attend to.' With a nine-and-a-half-year gap between Anne and Andrew, he and his youngest brother Edward are considered 'the second family' of the Queen and Prince Philip.

Andrew, named after his grandfather, Prince Philip's father, grew into a sturdy boy. At the age of eight he went to Heatherdown School near Ascot, strongly recommended to the Queen by an old boy, Angus Ogilvy, Princess Alexandra's husband. He is currently a pupil at Gordonstoun, where he is taking gliding lessons with the Air Training Corps at the nearby air base at Lossiemouth.

Andrew enjoys sailing with his family, and has a light aluminium craft which travels on a trailer when the family is at

left and right *In two scenes with father, the Princes Andrew and Edward use the roof of a Land Rover to advantage to spectate during horse trials; and eleven-year-old Prince Edward (right), the youngest child, joins Prince Philip in the driving seat of a horse and cart on a drive through Windsor Great Park.*

Balmoral. Known at school to his friends as 'Andy', the Prince is full of fun and popular, being more extrovert than his elder brother. In recent years he has grown rapidly to be almost as tall as his father.

Four royal births were awaited in 1964. The Queen was expecting her fourth child, Princess Alexandra her first, and both Princess Margaret and the Duchess of Kent their second. On 10th March, a bulletin was posted outside Buckingham Palace stating, 'The Queen was safely delivered of a son at 8.20 this morning. Her Majesty and the infant Prince are both well.' Princess Alexandra's son, the first of the batch of royal births, had arrived ten days earlier.

With Edward, the Queen completed her family before reaching her thirty-eighth birthday. The two elder children were then fast growing up, and the two younger ones became a source of great pleasure to her and Prince Philip. Prince Edward, fair haired like his father and sister, became a pupil at Andrew's first boarding school, Heatherdown.

Taking lessons from the past, it is the wish of the Queen and

Prince Philip that their two younger children should be shielded as far as possible from the public gaze until they leave school. No photographs appeared of the boys' christenings, for example. When interviewed on television, Prince Philip discussed this matter by saying, 'You cannot have it both ways. We try to keep the children out of the public eye so that they can grow up as normal as possible. But if you are going to have a monarchy you have got to have a family, and the family's got to be in the public eye.' Some of the most attractive shots of the royal family in Richard Cawston's 1969 film showed a carefree picnic with the two young Princes much in evidence.

Prince Andrew, second in line to the throne, will probably be created a peer on reaching adulthood. His mother may then bestow on him the Dukedom of York, the traditional title for the sovereign's second son, and one which her father held before becoming King.

When Prince Edward grows up he too will probably become a Duke. A title previously held by a member of the royal family is usually chosen, but the Queen need not follow this tradition.

THE QUEEN MOTHER

One of the best-loved members of the royal family is Queen Elizabeth, The Queen Mother. Those who have met her speak of her vivacity, charm and the genuine interest she shows in whatever subject is being discussed, banishing any nervousness in those in the presence of a royal lady for the first time.

Before her marriage she was Lady Elizabeth Bowes-Lyon, the fourth daughter and ninth child of the fourteenth Earl of Strathmore and Kinghorne, head of one of Scotland's oldest families. She was born on 4th August 1900, at her parents' Hertfordshire home of St Paul's Walden Bury. One further child, David Bowes-Lyon, was born to complete the family two years later. He was the closest in age to Elizabeth and the two children grew up as inseparable companions. David's death in 1961 was a great blow to her.

Most of Lady Elizabeth's childhood was spent in the country, partly at Glamis Castle, Angus, which was, according to Shakespeare, the scene of Macbeth's murder of King Duncan. Glamis came to her family as dowry towards the end of the fourteenth century, when King Robert II's daughter Jean married his secretary Sir John Lyon. But the greater part of the time Elizabeth stayed at St Paul's Walden Bury, a Georgian house of red brick, where she delighted in playing in the beautiful grounds and woods. When only a month old, a new nannie arrived to take care of the children. This was Miss Clara Cooper Knight, known to the children as 'Allah', as the younger ones were unable to pronounce Clara.

When aged seven she attended a charity garden party at Glamis, one of the attractions being a palmist. Her French governess asked her whether the palmist had read her hand. 'Yes, but she was silly. She says I'm going to be a Queen when I grow up.' 'That you can't be,' answered Mademoiselle, 'unless they change the laws of England for you.'

The First World War broke out in 1914, on Lady Elizabeth's birthday. Glamis was converted into an army convalescent hospital, and as time progressed Elizabeth spent more and more of her time helping there. King George V's second son, Prince Albert, later to become George VI, was serving in the Navy. When hostilities were over, the paths of Elizabeth and Albert were soon to cross. Lord Farquhar invited them to a party in London. As they danced, the Prince told her that they had met years before at a children's party given by the Duchess of Buccleuch at Montagu House, London, where even as a five-year-old child Elizabeth must have left a deep impression

left The Queen Mother chats to Prince Andrew in a typical scene between grandmother and grandson.

on him. He remembered that this Scottish girl had given him cherries from her angel cake.

The visit by the Prince to Glamis followed, and it was not long before the young Duke of York, as his father had recently created him, realized he had fallen in love. He had to woo Lady Elizabeth for three years before she accepted his hand, however. Lady Strathmore wrote during the winter of 1922-3, 'It was the first time I have ever known Elizabeth really worried. I think she was torn between her longing to make Bertie happy and her reluctance to take on the big responsibilities which marriage must bring.' The King, anxious for their marriage, told his son, 'You'll be a very lucky fellow if she says yes'. After an engagement of three months, they married in Westminster Abbey on 26th April 1923.

The Duke and Duchess of York were given White Lodge in Richmond Park for their home, but as their duties in London increased it was eventually decided that it would be more convenient for them to move into the centre of town. The King had recently bought 145 Piccadilly, and he gave this house to them, but before it was ready for occupation, their first child, Princess Elizabeth, was born at 17 Bruton Street. This was Lord Strathmore's London home, from which the future Duchess had set off for her wedding just three years earlier.

In 1927, the Duke and Duchess of York were given their first important assignment: a tour of Australia and New Zealand, including the inauguration of Canberra as Australia's new capital. It grieved the Duchess to be parted from her young daughter for six months, but she was able to persuade one of her sisters to release Allah to look after the Princess. Allah's loyal service was broken only on her death in 1946.

When the Duchess gave birth to a second daughter, Princess Margaret Rose, at Glamis Castle on 21st August 1930, the event was hailed as the first royal birth in Scotland for three centuries. Miss Margaret Macdonald was engaged as assistant nannie, with the prime duty of looking after Princess Elizabeth, while Allah became responsible for the new arrival. This was the start of Elizabeth's attachment to 'Bobo', as she calls her, and she remains in the household today as the Queen's dresser.

King George V decided to give the Duke and Duchess the Royal Lodge in Windsor Great Park as their country home. Though it was then in a dilapidated condition, their hard work at weekends transformed the Lodge into a charming yet simple home, surrounded by beautiful gardens and woodlands. It became their home in 1931, and is still a favourite of the Queen Mother.

left *Glamis Castle, Angus, where the Queen Mother as Lady Elizabeth spent part of her childhood. This was the historic Scottish home of her parents, the late Earl and Countess of Strathmore.*

above *In a photograph taken at Glamis, Lady Elizabeth, aged nine, poses with her brother David, the youngest of the family, in fancy dress.*

above right *The engagement picture of Lady Elizabeth Bowes-Lyon and the Duke of York (later King George VI), taken on 18th January 1923.*

right *On her wedding day on 26th April 1923, the future Duchess of York leaves for Westminster Abbey from her parent's London home in Bruton Street.*

top *A honeymoon photograph of the Duke and Duchess of York in the lovely grounds of Polesden Lacey, Surrey.*

above *The new Duchess of York tries her hand at the coconut shy during a visit to Loughton, Essex, in July 1923.*

left *The christening photograph of Princess Elizabeth Alexandra Mary, our present Queen, taken at Buckingham Palace on 29th May 1926.*

right *On a visit to Balmoral in September 1923, the Duke and Duchess of York stand with Queen Mary with, on her right, her youngest surviving son, Prince George, later Duke of Kent.*

right *The scene in West-minster Abbey on 14th November 1973 as the Queen and Prince Philip, followed by the Queen Mother and the Princes Charles and Andrew, leave in procession down the nave on the occasion of Princess Anne's wedding to Captain Mark Phillips.*

left *On their first important assignment together the Duke and Duchess of York open the Federal Parliament in Canberra, the new capital of the Commonwealth of Australia in 1927, during their tour of Australia and New Zealand on behalf of King George V.*

In 1936, the abdication crisis changed the lives of the Duke and Duchess of York. Elizabeth became Queen Consort of King George VI while lying ill at 145 Piccadilly with a severe attack of tonsillitis. The family moved from their informal household into Buckingham Palace and Windsor Castle. It was typical of Queen Elizabeth that when the daughter of her original French governess came to teach her own children French, and confessed she was overawed with the family's new status, the Queen smiled and told her, 'Only circumstances change, Georgina. People stay the same'.

After all the splendour of the coronation, Queen Elizabeth found on her return to Buckingham Palace that she had lost her voice. She whispered to Allah, 'I'm so glad it's all over'.

In July 1938 the King and Queen paid the first state visit to Paris since 1914. It was also their first foreign visit since the accession. Then, in mourning for her mother, she wore white rather than black, which was unusual on a state visit. The French press headlined her as 'The best dressed Queen to visit the world's fashion centre'. Afterwards the President's wife, Madame Lebrun, wrote to her, 'I wish to assure your Majesty that you have won the heart of the whole of Paris'.

Another royal visit during which the King and Queen won great popularity was their thirty-day tour of Canada in May and June 1939, including three days in the United States. In Montreal, newspapers came out in banner headlines, 'Roi,

Reine Ont Reconquis Le Canada' (The King and Queen reconquer Canada). In her broadcast to Canadian women, the Queen spoke of '. . . this great and friendly continent . . .' The people of Washington and New York, seeing a British King and Queen in their midst for the first time, gave them a tremendous welcome, while the visit enabled the King to have urgent discussions with President Roosevelt on the Nazi menace to world peace. A well-known 'isolationist' senator congratulated the King, '. . . on being a very good Queen-picker'. Another senator exclaimed, 'Ma'am, you sure are a thousand times prettier than your portraits'.

The crisis with Germany was already several months old. On 27th September 1938, the Queen travelled to Clydebank to launch the world's largest liner, previously listed as Job Number 552, and later to become famous as the *Queen Elizabeth*. The King was unable to leave London to accompany her as arranged because of the critical situation. On the following day the Prime Minister, Neville Chamberlain, flew off to Munich to meet Hitler.

War came and Buckingham Palace was bombed nine times. Queen Elizabeth commented, 'I'm glad we've been bombed. It makes me feel I can look the East End in the face.' She and the King travelled to the worst blitzed areas throughout the country. As Churchill said, 'Many an aching heart found some solace in her gracious smile'. Unlike other members of the

far left *Princess Anne and her husband pose with some heavyweight companions during a tour of New Zealand in 1974.*

left *The Queen Mother is photographed in the grounds of Clarence House on the occasion of her seventy-fifth birthday on 4th August 1975. Her birthdays are generally quiet family affairs, but on this rather special day, messages of congratulation arrived by every post.*

below *In another special birthday photograph, the Queen poses with Prince Philip and her youngest son Prince Edward at Windsor Castle, on 21st April 1976, her fiftieth birthday.*

above *The Duke and Duchess of York visit the Colonial Exhibition in Paris in July 1931 to inaugurate British Week. Here they are seen entering the Temple of Angora*

right *Six months before King Edward VIII abdicated and the Duke of York succeeded as King George VI, the Duke and Duchess of York pose in the garden of the Royal Lodge, Windsor, in June 1936, with their daughters Elizabeth and Margaret.*

left *In a remarkable colour photograph taken in July 1941, Queen Elizabeth, now the Queen Mother, gives her children the Princesses Elizabeth and Margaret their lessons in the open air at Windsor Castle.*

royal family she never wore uniform, choosing the clothes which suited her best, as the King wished. Her duties in these wartime days often extended to sixteen or seventeen hours a day, and she seldom reached her bed before midnight.

After the happy marriage in 1947 of her elder daughter to Prince Philip, and the birth of her grandchildren, Charles and Anne, Queen Elizabeth experienced intense worry over her husband's illness, which culminated in his death in February 1952. As Queen Dowager she decided to be known as Queen Elizabeth, The Queen Mother, which was similar to the style adopted by her mother-in-law, Queen Mary, in widowhood. After her many years of stress and strain she sought to resume a normal life and take up the many interests for which she had had little time as Queen. She and her elder daughter, now the Queen, exchanged houses, she and Princess Margaret eventually taking up residence at Clarence House, though still retaining the Royal Lodge, which was full of happy memories. Here Princess Margaret and her fiancé, Antony Armstrong-Jones, now the Earl of Snowdon, were photographed on their engagement prior to their marriage in 1960.

While staying in the north of Scotland with her close friend, Lady Doris Vyner, the Queen Mother heard that the sixteenth-century Barrogill Castle, near John o'Groats, had been put up for sale and was in danger of being demolished. Wishing to have a home in an isolated part of the country, she decided to purchase this small, rambling castle with its winding staircases and magnificent views over the Pentland Firth. She was able

above left *In September 1940 Buckingham Palace was damaged by a bomb which fell near the Belgian Suite. Here the King and Queen inspect the debris. More damage occurred three days later when the chapel was destroyed.*

far left *Sharing in the experiences of the blitzed Londoners, Queen Elizabeth toured areas damaged by air raids in September 1940.*

above *The Castle of Mey, Caithness. The Queen Mother bought this ancient castle on the northernmost tip of Scotland's mainland near John O'Groats in her widowhood, and after its restoration, moved in during October 1955.*

right *The Queen Mother talks with a group of Maori women at Rotorua, North Island, during her tour of New Zealand in 1966.*

to move in during October 1955, having restored the original name, Castle of Mey. 'It is a delight to me that I have a home in Caithness, a county of such beauty,' she said at Wick, when she received the Freedom of the Burgh.

The Queen Mother's other Scottish property is the small house of Birkhall, near Balmoral. Here she indulges in her favourite pursuit of fishing, particularly in the spring, when the River Dee is at its best. Her love of fishing goes back to her childhood days, but it is only in recent years that she has taken up salmon fishing.

The Queen Mother's love of racing is proverbial. Through friendship with the late Lord Mildmay, the outstanding amateur rider, she and Princess Elizabeth jointly purchased *Monaveen*, the nine-year-old Irish bred jumper, which they raced in her daughter's colours. This was a successful investment as the horse won in prize money three times its initial cost, but sadly it met with an accident at Hurst Park and had to be destroyed. After Lord Mildmay was drowned in 1950, the Queen Mother bought two horses from his stable, of which *Manicou* became a winner at Kempton Park that year. This was the first time a horse in the Queen's colours had won a race since the time of Queen Anne. Peter Cazalet, who had trained for Lord Mildmay, continued to be the Queen Mother's principal jumping trainer until his death in 1973. As an owner she is mainly interested in steeplechasing, although she has had several flat race winners and, like her daughter, is intensely interested in horse breeding. She attends as many race meetings as she can manage, and is an avid reader of *Sporting Life*. Every year she holds a party at Clarence House for her racing friends, including her trainers, jockeys, head lads and their predecessors. When entertaining racing enthusiasts to dinner she likes to decorate the table with her racing cups.

The Queen Mother takes a great interest in the past, and this is reflected in her love of pictures, antiques and silver. She started her personal collection after her marriage, and has made additions ever since. Her paintings, as well as old masters, include French impressionists and works by Augustus John, Graham Sutherland, Seago and Lowry. She reads a lot, enjoys watching television, plays the piano, and spends much of her spare time out of doors. Her love of gardening stems from her childhood, for her mother, Lady Strathmore, was a knowledgeable botanist.

All these activities have to be fitted into a tight schedule. The Queen Mother's many duties result in her spending most of her time at Clarence House, though she frequently visits countries abroad. Not everything goes according to plan, and the contretemps which occasionally occur amuse her, as do some of the press notices. One which caused her some merriment concerned her launching of HMS *Ark Royal* and it read as follows: 'On the dais stood the Queen, chatting to the bishop and waving to the crowds. Suddenly, silently she was in the sea, surrounded by a mass of broken wreckage and the comments of the dockyard workers.'

As well as two or three visits a year to her Castle of Mey, the Queen Mother usually spends weekends at the Royal Lodge, Windsor Great Park. When the royal family is at Balmoral in August and September, she goes to Birkhall, where she gives a party for her grandchildren. These now total six, four of the Queen and two of Princess Margaret, and they are all especially dear to her.

Elizabeth became Queen Mother at the age of fifty-one, considerably younger than her two predecessors, and she continues to get through a formidable amount of work, echoing the words of her late husband: 'We are not a family. We are a firm'. She celebrated her seventy-fifth birthday in 1975, and received congratulations from all over the world.

left *In another scene from her New Zealand tour of 1966, the Queen Mother relaxes from public ceremonies by trying her luck for trout at lake Wanaka in South Island.*

right *A royal family occasion at the Royal College of Music. The Queen, as patron, presents the honorary degree of Doctor of Music to her mother, president of the college, in December 1973.*

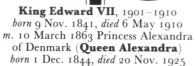

King Edward VII, 1901–1910
born 9 Nov. 1841, *died* 6 May 1910
m. 10 March 1863 Princess Alexandra
of Denmark (**Queen Alexandra**)
born 1 Dec. 1844, *died* 20 Nov. 1925

*2 brothers and
3 sisters*

King George V, 1910–1936
born 3 June 1865, *died* 20 Jan. 1936
m. 6 July 1893 Princess Mary of Teck
(**Queen Mary**)
born 26 May 1867, *died* 24 March 1953

Mary, Princess Royal
born 25 April 1897,
died 28 March 1965
m. 28 Feb. 1922,
**Henry, Earl of
Harewood**

2 sons

**Henry,
Duke of Gloucester**
born 31 March 1900
died 10 June 1974
m. 6 Nov. 1935
**Lady Alice Montagu
Douglas Scott**.
born 25 Dec. 1901

Prince William
born 18 Dec. 1941, killed
in a flying accident
28 Aug. 1972

**Richard, Duke of
Gloucester**
born 26 Aug. 1944,
m. 8 July 1972
Birgitte van Deurs

**Alexander,
Earl of Ulster**
born 24 Oct. 1974

King Edward VIII,
Jan.–Dec. 1936
born 23 June 1894, *died* 28 May 1972
abdicated 10 Dec. 1936 and created
Duke of Windsor 8 March 1937
m. 3 June 1937 Mrs Wallis Warfield

King George VI, 1936–1952
born 14 Dec. 1895, *died* 6 Feb. 1952
m. 26 April 1923 Lady Elizabeth Bowes
Lyon (**Queen Elizabeth The Queen
Mother**)
born 4 Aug. 1900

**The Princess
Margaret**
born 21 Aug. 1930,
m. 6 May 1960,
**Antony, Earl of
Snowdon**

**David,
Viscount Linley**
born 3 Nov. 1961

**Lady Sarah
Armstrong-Jones**
born 1 May 1964

Queen Elizabeth 1952–
born 21 April 1926
m. 20 Nov. 1947

THE ROYAL FAMILY TREE

The royal family tree indicates the Queen's descent from
Queen Victoria and also her relationship to her husband
Prince Philip, Duke of Edinburgh, and other members of the
royal family: both the Queen and Prince Philip are great-great-
grandchildren of Queen Victoria. For clarity not all Victoria's
descendants are included.

Queen Victoria 1837–1901
born 24 May 1819, *died* 22 Jan. 1901
m. 10 Feb. 1840
**Prince Albert of Saxe-Coburg and Gotha
(Prince Consort)**
born 26 Aug. 1819, *died* 14 Dec. 1861

*3 brothers and
4 sisters*

The Princess Alice
born 25 April 1843, *died* 14 Dec. 1878
m. 1 July 1862, **Grand Duke Louis IV
of Hesse**

George, Duke of Kent
born 20 Dec. 1902,
killed on active
service 25 Aug. 1942
m. 29 Nov. 1934
**Princess Marina
of Greece**
born 30 Nov. 1906,
died 27 Aug. 1968

The Prince John
born 12 July 1905,
died 18 Jan. 1919

*2 brothers and
4 sisters*

Princess Victoria
born 5 April 1863, *died* 24 Sept. 1950
m. 30 April 1884, Admiral of the Fleet,
Prince Louis of Battenberg,
later **Marquess of Milford Haven**

Edward, Duke of Kent
born 9 Nov. 1935,
m. 8 June 1961,
Katharine Worsley

Princess Alexandra
born 25 Dec. 1936
m. 24 April 1963,
the Hon. Angus Ogilvy

Prince Michael
born 4 July 1942

**George,
Earl of
St. Andrews**
born 26 June 1962

**Lord Nicholas
Windsor**
born 25 July 1970

**Lady Helen
Windsor**
born 28 April 1964

James Ogilvy
born 29 Feb. 1964

Marina Ogilvy
born 31 July 1966

*1 brother and
1 sister*

Admiral of the Fleet
**Louis, Earl
Mountbatten
of Burma**
born 25 June 1900
m. 18 July 1922,
**the Hon. Edwina
Ashley**
(*died* 21 Feb. 1960)

Princess Alice
born 25 Feb. 1885, *died* 5 Dec. 1969
m. 7 Oct. 1903, **Prince Andrew of
Greece**

**The Prince Philip,
Duke of Edinburgh**
born 10 June 1921

4 sisters

Charles, Prince of Wales
born 14 Nov. 1948

The Princess Anne
born 15 Aug. 1950
m. 14 Nov. 1973, Captain Mark Phillips

The Prince Andrew
born 19 Feb. 1960

The Prince Edward
born 10 March 1964

Acknowledgements

Colour

Camera Press 1, 20, 67 bottom, 68, 85 bottom, 86/87, 128 top, 128 bottom, 146/147, 147 bottom, 148; Fox Photos 2, 45, 46, 48, 66, 105 bottom, 125 bottom, 126/127, 166, 167 top; Keystone Press Agency 167 bottom; Serge Lemoine 106 top, 107 top; London Express News and Feature Services 47, 65, 67 top; Radio Times Hulton Picture Library/Studio Lisa 168; John Scott 19 top, 19 bottom, 85 top, 88, 105 top, 106 bottom, 107 bottom, 108, 125 top, 145, 147 top, 165.

Black and white

Aerofilms 110/111; Australian Information Service, London 33 top, 60, 61 top, 78, 79, 137 left; British Tourist Authority 171 top; Camera & Pen International 6/7; Camera Press 4, 14 top, 28, 75 bottom, 121, 149 top, 154 top; Central Press Photos 8, 38 bottom, 42 bottom, 44 top, 57, 62 top, 62/63, 70, 72/73 bottom, 111 top, 140 top, 144 bottom, 150 top, 162 bottom, 164; Country Life 160; Fox Photos 25, 30, 31 bottom, 34, 42 top, 54/55, 60/61 bottom, 69, 81, 89 top, 97 bottom, 102, 104, 109, 111 centre, 116 top, 116 bottom, 136 bottom; Graphic Photo Union 142; High Commissioner for New Zealand 32 top, 32/33 bottom, 59 bottom, 90/91, 171 bottom, 172; Information Canada Photothèque 43, 44 bottom, 49 top; Keystone Press Agency 27, 31 top, 39, 58 left, 64 top, 71 bottom, 75 top, 83, 89 bottom, 94, 95 bottom, 97 top, 111 bottom, 124, 139 bottom, 143 bottom; Serge Lemoine 92/93, 95 top, 96, 112 left; Ministry of Defence 113, 114, 138 top left, 138 top right, 138 bottom, 139 top, 140 bottom right, 150 centre, 150 bottom, 155; Odhams Books 11 bottom, 21 top; Popperfoto 10 top, 55 top, 56 bottom, 117 right, 161 top right, 162 top, 162 centre, 170 top; Press Association 10 bottom, 53, 72 top, 74 top, 76 top, 76 bottom, 98, 101, 122/123, 149 bottom, 162/163, 173; Radio Times Hulton Picture Library 12 bottom, 16 bottom, 18, 21 bottom, 35, 115, 117 left, 134, 161 top left, 161 bottom, 169 top, 169 bottom, 170 bottom; Eileen Ramsey 58/59; John Scott 112 right, 135, 141, 156, 158; Sport and General Press Agency 12 top, 38 top, 99, 130, 140 bottom left, 144 top, 150/151; Studio Lisa 9; Syndication International 6, 13, 14 bottom, 24, 26 left, 26 right, 29, 37 top, 37 bottom, 41 bottom, 49 bottom, 51, 52, 56 top, 64 bottom, 71 top, 73 top, 77, 80, 82, 84, 91 top, 100, 131, 132/133, 152/153, 154 bottom, 157; The Times 11 top, 15, 16 top, 16/17, 22/23, 36, 40, 41 top, 50, 118, 119 top, 119 bottom, 120, 136 top, 143 top; United Press International 137 right.

The photographs used in the royal family tree on pages 174/175 were supplied by Basano and Vandyk, Camera Press, Mansell Collection, National Portrait Gallery and Popperfoto.